On Golden Ground

Our Journey to the Eldorado

TRICIA BROWN

By Yukon Yonda and Dexter Clark

Larson & Larrigan, Publishers

Fairbanks ☼ *Anchorage*

Dedicated to those who blazed the trail . . .

—Y.Y. & D.C.

Many thanks to the Binkley family and to the Eldorado Gold Mine for the opportunity to share mining technique and history with visitors and locals alike. We'd also like to acknowledge pioneering Alaskan miners Ernie Wolff, Joe Vogler, Elder "Liberty" Lebert, C.J. Berry, and Harold Going. The rest of you know who you are.

Editor: *Tricia Brown*
Cover design / map: *Penny Panlener*
Cover photo: *Ken Graham/Ken Graham Agency*
Proofreader: *Kristen Olsen*
Color separations: *Norstar Color*
Printer: *Northern Printing*

Address inquiries to: Larson & Larrigan, Publishers
13671 Karen Street
Anchorage, AK 99515

Library of Congress Catalog Card Number: 97-70712

ISBN 0-9657676-0-4

PRINTED IN THE UNITED STATES OF AMERICA

First printing, May 1997

10 9 8 7 6 5 4 3 2 1

Contents

A pair of sourdoughs check the pan for "color" in this sixty-year-old image from the archives of Alaska magazine.

Introduction
By Tricia Brown

One hundred years ago, the Klondike was invaded by an army of gold-seekers, many of whom left comfortable lives as accountants, clerks, and business-men to join seasoned veterans in the Gold Rush. A fraction of the hundred thousand who set out for the North Country made it here. Of those, few became rich. Thousands turned back, broken physically or financially. Still more came, too heady with their dreams to heed the odds. Gold fever had taken over better judgment.

I remember reading the hundred-year-old letters of one such stampeder when I was editor of *Alaska* magazine. A young man named Rufus Simpson had come to Alaska, leaving a wife and two little boys back in California. His early letters were filled with optimism. Later, fatigue and doubt crept in. After a year, he repeatedly promised he'd come home soon — earnest promises that he made and broke, again and again. Even when Simpson was overcome by poor health and poverty, news of a possible strike or hearsay of somebody's good fortune lifted his spirits and grieved his wife's. Simpson did make it home eventually, but his health continued to decline, and he died within months.

Those who stayed in the northland tramped from the Yukon to Nome to Fairbanks to Iditarod, and on to many other minor strikes, each desperate to find his own Eldorado, unable to let go of hope. Many Far North cities can trace their roots to settlements that sprang up in the search for yellow metal. Fairbanks is one of them.

It's been a century, but the fever is as catchy as ever, and they're still extracting gold from this ground. Yukon Yonda and Dexter Clark were inflicted with the bug decades ago. Separate paths brought each of them to Fairbanks in the 1970s. Both were young single people ready for the romance, adventure, and challenges of the North. They discovered it all in the sweeping beauty of Alaska, in gold mining, and in each other.

Together, the Clarks have given many years of their lives to the back-breaking labor required of miners — establishing a remote camp in the Circle Mining District, hauling in supplies, water, fuel, and heavy equipment, then hauling it all out again at the end of the season. When Yukon wasn't in the cab of a bulldozer, she was cooking for a small army of miners, or inventing creative ways to do laundry without running water. Dexter moved dirt, and lots of it, at the controls of a backhoe or bulldozer. He learned a lot about geology, and which deposits most likely held gold. As camp mechanic, he discovered clever ways to fix heavy equipment, knowing that every hour the machines were idle was money out of their pockets.

The Clarks' mom-and-pop operation was shut down in the early 1980s when they did not meet new, stringent requirements of the Environmental Protection Agency. For a year, they ran a roadhouse known as the Central Lodge, cooking, tending bar, and putting up visitors in log cabin accommodations. Dexter was still chief mechanic, daily tending the diesel-fueled generator that served as their power source. On Sunday mornings, they opened up the lodge bar for the community's church meeting place.

Later, Yukon and Dexter returned to mining, digging on their own patented land just outside Fairbanks. At their Fox headquarters, a place they call

"The Biosphere," the Clarks live in a rustic, false-front home that looks like a Hollywood movie set for an Old West film. Beyond a lush vegetable garden, a small creek called Gold Run cuts through their back yard. In the overgrowth on the other side of the stream, a handful of buildings once stood near this stop on the Tanana Valley Railroad — Gilmore Station. Today, the tracks are gone, the structures have tumbled down, and rusted pieces of machinery litter the woods. The ground also holds much buried treasure. It's never been mined.

Near the creek stands the old cook shack, the twelve-by-twenty frame cabin that served as home and camp mess hall out on Harrison Creek twenty years ago. When Yukon and Dexter broke camp at the end of their final season in the Circle Mining District, they disassembled the building and moved it out with the rest of their heavy equipment. The shack traveled one hundred twenty miles along the Steese Highway to rest here. Today it's a guest house, heated by a wood stove, lit with kerosene lamps, and decorated with burlap potato sacks labeled "Yukon Gold."

Inside the Clark home, a movie poster of Klondike Kate hangs on one wall, and a bearskin rug is draped over the back of a '30s-era rocker. Along the window sills are small antique bottles in blue and green, and an ancient mammoth tusk, discovered when Dexter was digging for gold on their property. Rosie, the couple's Vietnamese pot-bellied pig, roams the kitchen, begging for food scraps.

With thirty-five combined years of mining Alaska's back country, Yukon Yonda and Dexter now spend their summers demonstrating modern mining techniques to visitors at the Eldorado Gold Mine, just north of Fairbanks on the Elliott Highway. At this Eldorado, visitors travel in narrow-gauge rail cars behind a replica of the original Tanana Valley Railroad engine that once traversed these parts.

Here, the Clarks proudly represent the community of Interior miners as they educate visitors about gold: where it's found, how it's used in industry and technology, how to pan it. But it's their own gold that gets attention. Eyes widen when Dexter opens his leather pouch, or poke, and several nuggets clank into his palm. A massive nugget hangs from each of their necks, and Yukon's fingers are studded with gold nugget rings. She's lost count of the times she's said: "Yes, it's real." And there's a story behind every nugget.

This first-person collection of stories written by my sister and brother-in-law — nuggets of life from Yukon Yonda and Dexter Clark — includes how they came to be gold miners, slices of life in a modern gold camp, crash landings, outlandish adventures with animals, and more. You won't soon forget these stories or the motto that they, and all the rest of Alaska's miners, swear by: *If it can't be grown, it has to be mined.*

A hundred years after the Klondike Gold Rush, the spirit that drew miners into this rugged way of life is unchanged. Like the stampeders on the Trail of '98, the Clarks have suffered hardship for their choices. They've weathered Alaska's boom-and-bust economy in their own pocketbooks, waited out long, harsh winters in anticipation of mining season, paid the doctor bills for physical ailments that are inevitable in such labor-intensive work. And still they mine.

They say they have to. ✿

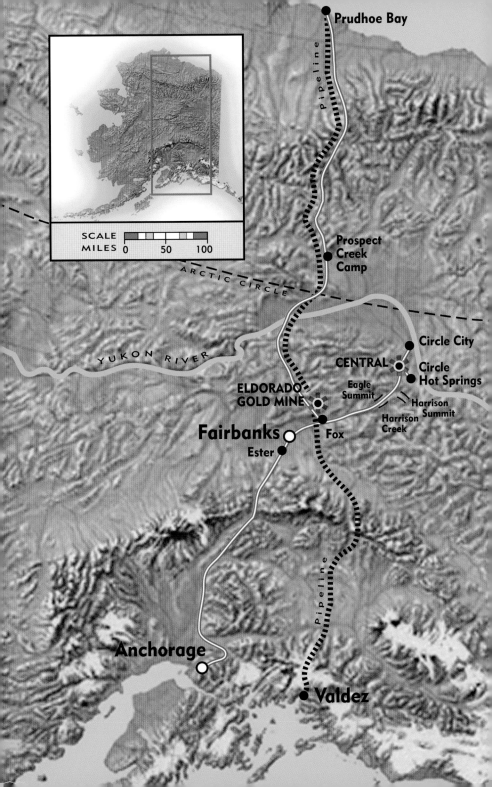

The Spell of the Yukon
By Robert Service

I wanted the gold, and I sought it;
*   I scrabbled and mucked like a slave.*
Was it famine or scurvy — I fought it;
*   I hurled my youth into a grave.*
I wanted the gold, and I got it —
*   Came out with a fortune last fall —*
Yet somehow life's not what I thought it,
*   And somehow the gold isn't all.*

No! There's the land. (Have you seen it?)
*   It's the cussedest land that I know,*
From the big, dizzy mountains that screen it
*   To the deep, deathlike valleys below.*
Some say God was tired when He made it;
*   Some say it's a fine land to shun;*
Maybe; but there's some as would trade it
*   For no land on earth — and I'm one.*

You come to get rich (damned good reason);
*   You feel like an exile at first;*
You hate it like hell for a season,
*   And then you are worse than the worst.*
It grips you like some kinds of sinning;
*   It twists you from foe to a friend;*
It seems it's been since the beginning;
*   It seems it will be to the end.*

I've stood in some mighty-mouthed hollow
*   That's plumb-full of hush to the brim;*
I've watched the big, husky sun wallow
*   In crimson and gold, and grow dim,*
Till the moon sets the pearly peaks gleaming,
*   And the stars tumbled out, neck and crop;*
And I've thought that I surely was dreaming,
*   With the peace o' the world piled on top.*

The summer — no sweeter was ever;
*   The sunshiny woods all athrill;*
The grayling aleap in the river,
*   The bighorn asleep on the hill.*

The strong life that never knows harness;
    The wilds where the caribou call;
The freshness, the freedom, the farness —
    O God! how I'm stuck on it all.

The winter! the brightness that blinds you,
    The white land locked tight as a drum,
The cold fear that follows and finds you,
    The silence that bludgeons you dumb.
The snows that are older than history,
    The woods where the weird shadows slant;
The stillness, the moonlight, the mystery,
    I've bade 'em good-by — but I can't.

There's a land where the mountains are nameless,
    And the rivers all run God knows where;
There are lives that are erring and aimless,
    And deaths that just hang by a hair;
There are hardships that nobody reckons;
    There are valleys unpeopled and still;
There's a land — oh, it beckons and beckons,
    And I want to go back — and I will.

They're making my money diminish;
    I'm sick of the taste of champagne.
Thank God! when I'm skinned to a finish
    I'll pike to the Yukon again.
I'll fight — and you bet it's no sham-fight.
    It's hell! — but I've been there before;
And it's better than this by a damsite —
    So me for the Yukon once more.

There's gold, and it's haunting and haunting;
    It's luring me on as of old;
Yet it isn't the gold that I'm wanting
    So much as just finding the gold.
It's the great, big, broad land 'way up yonder.
    It's the forests where silence has lease;
It's the beauty that thrills me with wonder,
    It's the stillness that fills me with peace.

Reprinted with permission of the Putnam Publishing Group from *The Collected Poems of Robert Service* © 1940 Robert Service.

A nice pan of rocks. This is what it's all about. After years of mining in remote Alaska, now we're digging closer to home.

Partners in Mining, Partners in Life

By Yukon Yonda and Dexter Clark

Most of the people you meet here in Alaska are from somewhere else, and we're no different. But you may be wondering: How did a guy from a Wisconsin

Lynette Stinson, 8

Dexter Clark, 7

dairy farm end up mucking for gold near the Arctic Circle? And who'd have thought he'd meet and marry a fellow Midwesterner — a camp cook and heavy equipment operator called Yukon Yonda?

Many people ask us if we live in Alaska year-round, how we ended up here, and why we went into gold mining. The short answers are "Yes," "Long story," and "Lots of reasons." But for the really curious, here's the long version:

Yukon:

I was almost six years old when I first saw Alaska from aboard the U.S.S. Frederick Funston. *My family was en route to Japan where my Dad was stationed in the post-war years. I remember thinking, "Wow!" as a peered out the porthole at Adak, an island in the Aleutian Chain.*

Although I never forgot Alaska, I didn't return

until September 19, 1975, when brother Mike, sister Terry, myself and two cats arrived in Fairbanks after a harrowing two-week trip on the Alcan, joining others of the Stinson family who'd come before us.

I had been corresponding with my father fairly regularly about their move to Alaska. He'd written me about the job opportunities with the Trans-Alaska Pipeline which was under construction, and ever looking after my single status, shared with me the fact that the men outnumbered the women 250 to 1.

I decided to go north, not for male companionship, but for the job possibilities. Which was a good decision. There's a saying here describing Alaskan men: "The odds are good but the goods are odd!" Within two weeks of my decision, I had contacted Mike and Terry, budgeted for the trip, quit my job, rid myself of excess belongings, and took off!

We drove from Chicago to Fairbanks in a 1964 Chevrolet that cost $75 — a real "Captain America" car that Mike had purchased just for the trip up the Alcan. We'd put new tires on all around and bought a brand new battery. I'd wanted the mechanic at Sears to put her up on a rack and install new shocks, but he refused, saying something about a really rusted frame.

By the time we all were ready to depart, the car looked like something out of Steinbeck's "Grapes of Wrath." As we drove away I remembered a very little girl, standing tippy-toed on a suitcase looking out a porthole in wonder.

The $75 Chevy made it, but not without lots of help. For that I owe a debt of gratitude to the Canadians who came to our rescue after we threw a rod in Alberta, a transmission just outside Edmonton and a radiator out in God-knows-where. Thanks just didn't seem enough when they wouldn't take any pay for their effort. I learned a valuable lesson about people of the North.

Within two days of our arrival, I landed a job bartending at Pike's Landing, located on the Chena River at the edge of town. From behind the bar, I met the rest of the state and fell deeper under Alaska's spell. Trappers coming through with stories of how the fur was moving. Miners getting their crews ready for the new season. Bush pilots constantly juggling cargo. Hunters looking for game. And folks that made the Far North seem normal, regular: the school teachers, the bookkeepers, "the butcher, the baker, and the candlestick maker" mix of what makes a community last.

During my first couple of years in town, I rented a place, but later I came across a tract of land and tried my hand at homesteading out in the community of Ester. About that time I also started looking for a cook's job in a remote mining camp.

Little did I know where it would lead me.

Dexter:

I grew up on a dairy farm in Wisconsin, something I've never regretted even though it meant lots of hard work. There were always chores to do, and the cows needed constant care. Farm life introduced me to operating and maintaining machinery, which came in very handy later.

In the early 1970s, my folks both passed away within a year of each other. My sister and her military husband were stationed in Alaska, and I decided to move up with them. We needed each other's help in handling our grief.

It was forty below zero when I landed in Fairbanks. Even in mourning, I sensed this was an exciting time and place to be. The oil pipeline was going to be built soon. The vastness of the land captivated me, and the prospect of making some big bucks in a few years was enough to get me to stay.

My first job was mopping floors in the downtown Safeway, what is now the Post Office. Before the next winter set in, I'd snagged a job as a school janitor. By February of '74, I was headed for Prospect Creek Camp as a radio telephone operator and weather observer on the construction route of the Trans-Alaska Pipeline.

The pipeline was to cross more than eight hundred miles of the state in a north-south course from Prudhoe Bay on the Beaufort Sea, to Valdez on Prince William Sound. Engineering and building the pipeline was an awesome achievement. But one saying especially summed up the lighter side of the experience: "Never have so many done so little for so much money."

Most of the pipeline workers would spend nine weeks at the remote camp and then take two weeks of rest and relaxation. My job required a rotation of four weeks on and two weeks off. It was during one of these R&Rs in the fall of 1975 that my road took a turn toward mining.

While shopping in the sporting goods department at J.C. Penney in Fairbanks, I met Dave, a fellow I recognized from high school in Milton, Wisconsin. I assumed he had a pipeline job, too. No, he said. He was working with a gold miner, "mining the rim pay" left by the old-timers. We went back to my apartment, where he pulled out a leather "poke," or pouch, containing the last cleanup: several hundred ounces of nice-looking gold nuggets. After a couple hours of hearing his mining stories and taking pictures of ourselves with the gold, for me the hook was firmly set.

In the summer of '76, I visited their mine whenever I could and became friends with Dave's partner, Sam. They even built an airstrip so I could fly in supplies when I visited. The next spring, during a visit to the base camp in Fairbanks, Sam asked me what I was going to do with all that money I'd made on the

My first visit to a gold mine on Harrison Creek, August 1976.

pipeline. I told him I was looking to buy a little gold.

"Why didn't you say something sooner?" he said. "I could show you how to dig that gold straight out of the ground." He would provide the mining claim and some support in exchange for fifteen percent of the gold. Earn while you learn. Gold was $80 an ounce.

On Sam's desk was a motto: "We live by the Golden Rule. The guy with the gold makes the rules." With that out of the way, my next question was: "How do you mine for gold?"

His answer was simple: "Just dig a hole in the ground and keep making it bigger."

So that summer, I bought a small track loader. With a track loader, you can scoop the gravel right up out of the stream bed and haul it to your sluice box. The sluice box was made from timbers and plywood since the materials were cheap and my welding skills were nil at that time. The sluice box was thirty inches wide with angle iron riffles along its forty-foot length. An old dump truck dump bed served as a hopper for dumping in the pay dirt. The entire creek was directed through the sluice by building dikes and dams. By experience, I learned about the importance of spillways, a way for excess water to get around the sluice box. The term "settling pond" became a part of my vocabulary.

Despite the mistakes of my first season, in 1978 I partnered up with my brother-in-law, Craig, who brought a small dozer into the deal. He was warned about mining. An old local grocer told him, "There is more money went into them hills than will ever come out."

We two greenhorns wondered if he wasn't right.

TRICIA BROWN

Ready to head for the creeks.

Yukon:

In the spring of '78, I was opening up the Red Garter Saloon in Ester and had put out word that I was looking for work as camp cook in a remote mining camp. My motivation was to eventually learn to operate and maintain the heavy equipment used in camp. I had two things in my favor: One, I am one darn good cook, and willing to work long hours. Two, growing up back in Kankakee, Illinois, I had acquired some mechanical ability and understanding of motors and engines.

By mid-May I'd received word a new mining crew needed a cook! Yahoo! I was hired! The crew would be working on Harrison Creek in the Circle Mining District, north of Fairbanks by a hundred thirty-five miles. The operation would be leasing the claim from another miner for a percentage of the gold removed in the season.

That first season for me was a baptism of fire. Lots to be learned and some of those lessons, hard ones. But it set my course and fulfilled my dream of what an Eldorado could bring.

Then along came Dexter Clark, whose journey also brought him from the Midwest and across my path. I met him at the end-of-season "Road Closing" mining party at the Arctic Circle Hot Springs. My life was forever changed after that night.

Dexter:
The old adage of "all work and no play" is exemplified by miners everywhere. They work hard. They play hard. The only places to play for hard-working placer miners of the Circle Mining District are the little town of Central and, just beyond town, Arctic Circle Hot Springs. But going to Central was a three-hour round-trip. You really had to want to go there.

First, you should know that the Steese Highway runs north and east of Fairbanks for a little more than a hundred fifty miles, ending at the Yukon River in the village of Circle. The highway has mileposts marking their respective distances from Fairbanks. These mile marker numbers are used in any conversation about the Steese. For example, pavement ends at 44 Mile. The Harrison Creek turn-off is at 114 Mile. Downtown Central and the junction with the Hot Springs road is about 126 Mile.

The narrow, often washed-out road to the mining camp on Harrison Creek winds eleven miles through creek bottoms, old tailing piles, and over a 4,300-foot summit. Generally speaking, it was about an hour's drive in a four-wheel-drive just to get from camp out to the Steese Highway.

After a minimum twelve hours of hard work, you might think the last thing someone would want to do was drive an hour and a half, one way, into "town." But consider that very few of the mining camps have showers or laundry facilities. Add the monotony of the same routine for long, long hours, blend in the

Our mining neighbors in the fall of '76 were known around the Circle Mining District as the "Harrison Creek Savages." From left is Dupa, Big Lip, and King Rat, the crew at Singing Sam's Rainbow Mine.

complete lack of social contact, put a pool table and a whiskey bottle at the end of that drive, and get your kids off the street. The later in the season it gets, the more appealing a trip.

It was a Saturday, late September of 1979, and termination dust (the first sign of snow, terminating summer) had already dusted the mountain tops around our mine. The crew was ready to mutiny unless we went "over to the Springs," and soon. An early quit meant we stopped mining at about six p.m., grabbed our grips with our shower stuff in them, and shot on over to Central.

Central Lodge was the first business establishment at the edge of town, and therefore the first stop. Cold beer and a pool table were added incentives.

After our thirst was partially quenched, we headed for the Hot Springs for a shower and a dip in the naturally heated outdoor pool. We pulled into the parking lot just as three women were getting out of another pick-up truck. As we all entered the bar, one of the women smiled at me and said, "Let's go play!"

I bought a couple rounds of drinks, and we introduced ourselves. She said her name was Lynette, but her friends all called her Yukon Yonda, and she'd like to kick my butt in a game of pool. After she won three games straight, I saw her standing beside an old piano bench looking at me like she was sizing me up. So I strolled over, got right in her face and said, "Well, at least I'm still taller than you."

Not exactly your every day pick-up line, I figured she was thinking. But it seemed to work. We shared the piano bench and began to talk more seriously. She told me about cooking for some miners who had ripped her off by not paying her. I told her they were the kind of people who were giving gold miners a bad name. Maybe I could use a new cook next season. I didn't mention that my crew was getting tired of their own cooking.

We hit it off well enough that she came back to the mine with us and demonstrated her culinary skills by fixing a picture perfect breakfast of sausage, eggs and toast. I was already so toasted that when she served me my meal, I gave what must have sounded like a disgusted snort, for I was challenged by Yukon: "If you don't want it, throw it out the window."

The window behind me had already been repaired once with clear plastic and duct tape, so it was real simple to accept the dare.

If I'd been hungry, things could have been different. In one fluid motion, I put my elbow through the plastic, dumped the beautiful plateful of food out the window and handed her the empty plate. The gauntlet had been dropped. This was the point at which our life together really began.

"I" became "we," for both of us.

Yukon*:*

In spite of our rocky beginning, Dexter hired me on as camp cook for the mining season of 1979. I'd be mining on the Harrison again, but with a new crew working further upstream on the North Fork.

Our staging area — where we geared up, packed, and loaded supplies and equipment for the move out to Harrison Creek — was in North Pole. A new cook shack had been built, all in pre-fab panels ready to be lag-bolted together. Lists were all checked and inventory adjusted to include a few more necessary items. Once you are out there, you can't simply run to Fairbanks if you have forgotten something. It just gets added to a list for the next trip to town.

I'd learned a lot from the previous mining season — ordering bulk supplies and remembering tricks for livening up a menu now and then.

In camp we would have a few creature comforts,

but for the most part, you've got to be your own tour guide. I allotted space in my packing for time-off projects, reading material, needlework and such. No TV or VCR, but we'd have a radio, and if somebody in town needed to reach us, there was a radio phone at Singin' Sam's Rainbow Mine just up the creek.

In that second season on the Harrison, my duties were expanded, as I had some experience under my belt. I was not only camp cook. I also assisted during clean-ups, became somewhat of a wrench jockey and welder, and finally learned to operate the camp equipment. I really enjoyed "feeding the box," dumping tons of pay dirt at the top of the sluice box.

Throughout our years in the mining industry, albeit a "ma and pa" operation, I've held dear the notion of being a contributor. Producing new wealth and tending the land at the same time.

My advice about getting into the minerals industry, gold mining in particular, is don't! There's a reason they call it a "fever." You will work long, hard hours. And no matter where you go or what you are doing, you won't quit looking for where the "pay lays," and I'm not talking soccer. Robert Service said it best in "The Spell of the Yukon":

> "I wanted the gold, and I sought it;
> I scrabbled and mucked like a slave.
> Was it famine or scurvy — I fought it;
> I hurled my youth into a grave.
> I wanted the gold, and I got it —
> Came out with a fortune last fall, —
> Yet somehow life's not what I thought it,
> And somehow the gold isn't all." ✿

TRICIA BROWN

Our partnership took a new dimension in August of 1981. In a toast to our future as a married couple, we raised our glasses in the Cook Shack alongside the stream known as Maiden Pup.

Ring of Fire
By Yukon Yonda

I'll never forget the summer of '81. We lost our fix on the paystreak sometime around the end of July. For a couple of weeks, the gold was just not coming out of the ground, no matter what intelligence or past experience we applied. In one cut, after forty hours of working the sluice box, we cleaned up a measly five ounces. The next cut, thirty hours, and three ounces in the sluice. Then, on top of no gold, our crew had decided to head for town. Nobly so, for they also realized our position. Our accountant agreed: Winnow it down, cut the expenses now. Things were tense. What hair Dexter had left, he was pulling out. Where had the gold gone?

We took inventory. There was plenty of diesel and other necessary fluids for the machines in camp. That was paid for. The equipment, regularly maintained, was running great. We had a good stock of food and supplies in general. And between the two of us, we were convinced that before long we'd find that elusive paystreak again. Things weren't so bad.

One day, convinced the "pay" was in the next bucket, we headed for the pit. Picking the next cut, Dexter started pushing overburden and I checked the dirt with the gold pan. Finally some pay started showing in the pan, enough to agree to dig here, but that didn't diminish the tension — was this the place? Would it pull us out of this rut?

Blame it on that tension, but for some reason,

Working a cut. Every time we paused, an argument erupted.

one that neither of us can remember, we started picking at each other. We were operating smoothly as a team, as usual. He pushed pay dirt to a stockpile near the box and I scooped it up in the four-yard bucket on the loader. Then I hauled it up the ramp to dump into the sluice for washing. But at about every third push I met Dexter at the stockpile. Each time, his blade was down and he was standing on the tracks, waiting to say something to me. Each time, I stopped my machine and stepped out onto the loader tire, aggravated and ready to work, not talk.

The spittin' match escalated with every stop. There we were squabbling like a couple of kids, shouting at each other only to return to our machines and proceed moving the dirt. After the last episode, I climbed back in the loader, thinking, *God, I'm acting like a shrew; red-faced with anger, veins standing out on my neck!* Then again, we met at the stockpile. Once more I got out of the loader, ready to confront that dragon on the other side of the pile. But this time something had changed. I could see a difference in Dexter. *Apparently he's been considering our conduct, too,* I thought, *and he's about to apologize.* Boy, was I in for a surprise. In a calm voice he called out over the roar of the engines:

"Will you marry me?"

You could have pushed me over with a feather! Hearing his question, I instantly pictured me, veins sticking out of my neck, spittle flying out of my mouth, this monster standing on the loader tire.

"You want to marry *me*?!" I asked in complete astonishment.

"Yes," he said, "Set the date."

"Okay," I yelled back. "August twenty-third."

And we resumed our work with entirely different thoughts traveling through our minds.

When Dexter and I met more than a year earlier, marriage was the farthest thing from each of our minds. By now, however, we'd had two seasons of working together, learning each day, sharing good and bad during a time of great change in the mineral industry, and in Alaska's mining community. Shouldering life together, and biting back when necessary, gave each of us the opportunity to see the other standing on his or her principles. We'd each grown to admire and love the other as a life partner. Marriage seemed the natural course.

We decided to share our vows right there at our mining camp at the confluence of the North Fork of Harrison Creek and Maiden Pup, just a few claims below the camp for Singin' Sam's Rainbow Mine.

A week before the wedding, we made a trip to Fairbanks for camp supplies, and we selected simple gold wedding bands for each other. We had to have them sized, however, so the jeweler said he'd mail them to Central.

When the mail plane came in a few days later, I met it to pick up the rings. Next on my list — a trip over to the Hot Springs to have a talk with Bob LaRude. Marching in the door, I told Bob I was there for one purpose only: *I wanted the piano bench from his saloon.*

"If I have to beg, borrow or steal the bench, I don't care," I said. "But when I leave, it's going with me!"

Bob knew about the "goings on" over on the Harrison in a couple of days and he had a good reason to say yes to my plea.

It had been just over a year when Dexter and I, both in town from different camps, had come to Arctic Circle Hot Springs for a soak in the hot mineral water of their Olympic-sized pool. We also each knew Bob had live music in the bar that night. Oh, we'd bumped into each other in the parking lot and seen each other at the pool. We'd even shot some eight-ball on the pool table. (Need I remind you that I beat him three games straight?) But sitting side by side on that bench is where we met. So Bob LaRude's wedding gift to the two of us was the use of that bench again — this time for our vows.

Mission accomplished! With the box containing our wedding rings from the mail plane in the front seat, and the piano bench in the back of the truck, I headed for the creek and Maiden Pup camp.

Our wedding day, August 23, 1981, began early with Dexter up and out of the cook shack and down to the pit. Wedding or not, there was mining to be done. Everything else was pretty much ready.

All I had to do that morning was clean away our breakfast leavings and ready the cabin for the afternoon celebration. I had to wash the dishes, burn the trash, do a little dusting, set up the reception table, and put some finishing touches on the cake decorations. Then I'd make time for me to relax and "dress" for my wedding.

We'd picked up the marriage license on our last supply run to Fairbanks. And we'd each bought a brand new pair of Carhartt pants — tan, very heavy canvas, work wear. Dexter and I figured starting our married life in some good work clothes would be smarter than

TRICIA BROWN

*I kidnapped the piano bench from Arctic Circle Hot Springs for
our outdoor wedding. It was on that bench that we first met.*

investing in a wedding gown and tuxedo.

After finishing the breakfast dishes, and taking
care of my other chores, I gathered up the trash. As I
was going out the cook shack door, I noticed the cardboard box that the jeweler had used to mail our rings.
Inside among all the foam peanuts was one black velvet
ring box holding Dexter's ring. I looked for the other
one with my ring in it, but I couldn't find it. *He must
have taken it with him to the pit,* I thought. *How truly
sweet and romantic.* With that, I swept the cardboard
box into the trash can, along with some of the peanuts
that had fallen onto the table during my search for the
other ring case. Then out the door to the burn barrel. A
little diesel, a match, and that chore was complete.

Friends had started to arrive. Folks that had dri-
ven up the Steese Highway from Fairbanks had bumped
over a long, gravel road for more than a hundred miles,
and some of them in vehicles best left at home. Mike
Carter, the marriage commissioner and owner of Central
Lodge, came over and down Harrison Summit with very

little brakes, much paler for the experience.

Tim McKay, an independent trucker and friend who has hauled most of our mining outfit for years, showed up with a gallon of Crown Royal and cookies. Another miner friend, Rollie Achman, was asked to give the bride away. His brother, Singin' Sam, brought the champagne and stood in as best man. My maid of honor, Jasmine, brought the bridal flowers from a friend's greenhouse in Central. My brother Mike, sister Tricia, and her friends Perry and Ben were there to represent the family of the bride.

I was ready. I'd baked the wedding cake, and iced down the refreshments with the last of the creek glacier leftovers. A sprig of flowers was pinned in my hair.

Dexter had come back from the pit, washed up, and changed. Beneath his open flannel shirt was a T-shirt with a cartoon of a pig reclining on a quarter moon, and the words: "Swine on Harvest Moon." Scrubbed and combed, and swirling the glacier ice in his drink, he was anxious for the ceremony to begin.

Even though it was only mid-August, the leaves already were beginning to turn in the hills around the creek, and the view outside the cook shack was a picture of majesty when Mike, the marriage commissioner, called for everyone to gather 'round.

Dexter and I took our seats on the piano bench and Mike began. When he asked if anybody there would speak against this union, there was a long, silent pause.

"Whew," he said, wiping his forehead, "I really thought I'd get an answer!" The laughter relaxed us, and he continued with the traditional vows going to me first. I, of course, answered yes to all of the above, took Dexter's hand, and slipped the ring on his finger.

Then it was Dexter's turn to repeat the vows. He looked into my eyes and said, "I will if you will!" We both turned back to Mike, who was almost to the part of doing some "pronouncing" when I called a stop to the whole proceedings.

"Wait just a minute here!" I looked back at Dexter and asked, "Where's my ring?"

Most of the congregation hadn't heard my question, but the look on Dexter's face told me all. He was completely buffaloed. I read it in his eyes: I'd picked up the rings in Central. I had secured them in the cook shack two days ago, and he knew better than to touch them. My hand flew to my mouth as I turned to stare at the burn barrel. I had torched my own wedding ring!

For once in my life, I couldn't get any words out. I could only stare as I mentally kicked myself in the butt. Then my new husband put his arm around me, and I knew everything was all right.

The marriage commissioner came to the rescue. Before the wedding, Mike had been disappointed to learn that we both had rings, that he'd have to break his long-standing tradition of fashioning a $100 bill as the bride's ring. Moments later, when he got back to pronouncing us man and wife, he did so while Dexter slipped a brand new $100 bill ring on my finger.

Then the party moved into the cook shack, and everyone got in the liars' line — sharing memories that included us but were really about mining. Soon the cake was cut, and we opened presents. One was a gift certificate for an overnight stay in the honeymoon suite at Arctic Circle Hot Spring with a hot tub in the room and Eggs Benedict served in bed the next morning. We also were told that Bob LaRude and his wife were planning a reception for us the next day in the saloon! Well, it looked as though our "dance card" was full, and no mining would be going on tomorrow. Our remaining crew volunteered to operate while we were gone, but we decided everyone would go for the fun.

The next morning, I still had one thing on my

TRICIA BROWN

The bride and groom each wore new Carhartt work clothes, and the marriage commissioner's "tuxedo" was really a T-shirt.

mind: To find my wedding ring before we headed over the summit for the reception.

I retrieved a No. 4 screen from the camp clean-up area, moved the front-end loader next to the burn barrel, and lowered the bucket. My plan was to screen the ashes into the bucket until I found the ring. If it didn't show up in the screen, I could run this material through the main sluice. I dug in with my bare hands, handful after handful of ash, separating out cans as I went.

Time ran out on me. Covered in ash, and literally hitting the "bottom of the barrel," I went in to clean up, disappointed, but excited to be going to Central.

We piled into the old Dodge for the trip to the Hot Springs. That afternoon, the saloon was full of well-wishers. At evening's end, we sent our crew home and promised to show up for work fairly early the next day. Can't let this wedding eat up any more mining time.

Back in camp, I immediately resumed my mission of finding that darn wedding ring, and we ran the burn barrel material through the main sluice. One dump of the loader bucket took care of that. Next we shut the water down and examined the top few riffles. There it was, two riffles down!

It was no longer a beautiful round gold band. In the burn barrel, the temperatures had been high enough to melt the gold into a little gold ball. Rolling in my palm, the size of a BB, was my wedding "ring."

After sixteen years of marriage, I still carry that piece of gold buckshot, and I wear the band purchased by the $100 dollar bill that Dexter had placed on my finger that day. We've gone on to find more gold, but nothing ever as big and as bright as the life we've shared in the goldfields. ✿

TRICIA BROWN

In the mining game, there's no shortage of philosophers.

High Life on Harrison Creek
By Dexter Clark

Living in a mining camp, seeing the same people day-in and day-out, on the job and off . . . well, personal relationships tend to undergo a test. The person you think is a great guy in town can be transformed by isolation. You find out a lot about yourself and the fellows working around you. Many a cold fall night has found a group of miners sitting around the barrel stove, chocked full of wood, a beer or drink in hand, discussing just about anything you can imagine.

In one of these late night philosophical discussions, the subject of aloneness, not loneliness, came up. Somebody posed the question: *What is the longest period of time you have spent totally by yourself?* Then the qualifiers: really alone, no radio, no TV, no books or magazines to comfort you, absolutely alone. Rare, even in this area of acknowledged isolation is the individual who can say so much as twenty-four hours. The natural flow of this conversation then turned to: *Who are we, then?* A composite of all the people we have known, the events we have seen, the places we been, and the stories we have heard. In short, the product of our environment.

One night, right after the barrel stove was refueled and the glasses refilled, came another question to cause us to search our souls: *What would you do if you found a nugget as big as that barrel stove?* Some of the answers were obvious: Quit mining and move far away from this God-forsaken frozen tundra to someplace where it never snows, and they never heard of diesel fuel. Invest the money from selling the nugget and live happily ever after off the earnings. One grizzled old mechanic told how he would buy all the newest equipment available and use any cash left over to "keep mining until it was all gone."

My answer was a little different: "The first thing is, I wouldn't tell anyone about it." I watched my friends react to this new line of thinking. Indeed, showing off and bragging about a big nugget was usually the first thing you did when you found one. Their quizzical looks changed to understanding as I continued.

"Because if word got out about a nugget that big, sooner or later someone would come along who'd want you to donate it to a museum." These words brought knowing nods all around. We'd all heard of many nice nuggets ending up behind glass.

"Can you imagine what it would take to even move a nugget that big?" By now it was evident to my audience that I had really given this some thought. I continued: "I'll tell you what I'd do. I'd take pictures of that nugget, and then I'd build a simple cabin over it. Whenever Yukon and I needed supplies or a vacation, I would saw off a hunk of gold to sell. We'd take pictures of all the fun we had spending the money, and when it was all gone, we'd donate the pictures to the museum."

With that seed planted, the conversation turned to estimates of just how much a nugget that big would weigh, and if there would really be any way to move it. Before the drinks were drained again, they all agreed that my plan was the only practical one.

So with each of us hoping that a golden boulder would become more than the stuff of a friendly fireside fantasy, we turned to our beds and our dreams.

Since that night, I will always wonder: *If any of them found one, would they even tell me about it?* ✿

Gold Is Where You Find It
By Yukon Yonda and Dexter Clark

Yukon:

Living in a mining camp in the Bush for five months of the year can seriously change your point of view about the creature comforts we take so lightly. Depending on how new the camp is, food must be kept cold by caching in the creek or, if you're lucky, in a propane refrigerator. There's no city water or sewer. No phones, no newspapers, no television, no videos. No switch to flip for electric light. Kerosene or propane meets that need, and besides, the sun stays in the sky for most of the day in the summer. *Who can complain?*

Every day certain things just have to be done, and there's nobody else to do them but you. Starting with the cooking, there's three meals a day plus snacks, rain or shine. And some of those meals are packed and sent to the pit so the crew doesn't have to travel back to the cook shack. Juggling the time! The list of chores seemed endless sometimes. At camp, I baked bread every other day, usually four

Besides serving as camp cook and medic, I also hung out a barber sign in 1979.

to six loaves, plus a mix of pastries and desserts to add to the menu. Baking treats everyday is most enjoyable because it means time to relax, read or just plan old lounge in the sun. A cake in the oven is thirty-five to forty golden minutes of lovely leisure.

And then there's the never-ending chore that has

to be done before you can even begin the cooking, cleaning, or washing: hauling water. During my first mining season, I learned that even in the middle of nowhere, you can still have running water. Me and my buckets. I ran it in, and I ran it out.

At the start of season, my fill spot for fresh water was very close to camp, very convenient. As the mining progressed up the creek, so did the distance to clean, clear water. By mid-season the distance grew to the length of a football field — and so did my arms. Carrying two five-gallon buckets each trip, I thought by the end of season my forearms would look like Popeye.

When laundry day came around, I told the crew members my deal: I'd wash, hang dry, fold and deliver clean laundry, but I'd get to keep the fine gold that washed out of the really "mucky" work clothes.

As a bonus, I'd also get to spend the day in town. Actually in the backyard of the Central Roadhouse. Mike Carter, the lodge owner, had set up an old wringer-washer on a plywood pallet and had run a hose and an extension cord to this wonderful convenience. The clotheslines were nearby, as was the bar, the restaurant (somebody else's cooking), the phone and the television. After just a couple of months in the Bush, laundry day in Central, with running water and electricity, was like spending a day in heaven.

And I had a pretty good system for getting this job done. First all the white bedclothes and underwear were washed, rinsed, and hung up to dry in the sun. Under normal circumstances when you're ready to drain this type of washer, you just unhook and drop the drain hose, then start filling it for the next load. Instead, I used the same wash water, along with another cup of soap, to start the dirtiest load. When that was finished agitating and feeding through the wringer into the rinse water, I let the water settle for a few minutes then lowered the drain hose just enough to slowly drain most of the water. With about two to four inches of water remaining, I turned the machine on its side and scooped out the residual mud on the bottom of the tub. That material was put into a jar for panning once I got back to camp. That first season I got out almost a full ounce of fines from the wringer washer. Mining the miner!

The camp cook shack that year was a Winnebago that served as my quarters, the pantry, and the mess hall for the crew's meals. A delightful place, but fairly crowded at mealtimes and during after-shift cribbage games.

I had grown up in a large family, and being the second oldest I learned to cook for lots of people early. What I didn't know was how to order in bulk and how to relate that to long-term menu planning. Every three weeks, the camp foreman would make a trip to town, and sometimes supplies didn't make it back right away. I quickly learned to always have extra staples on hand, and where to stash candy bars to surprise the crew now and then.

Luckily the Winnebago had refrigeration, and the cook stove was propane, which reminds me of another hard lesson that first season. When supplying the cook list for the trip to town, I forgot to order an extra propane bottle to get me through till supplies arrived, so I learned the hard way. For three days I cooked all the meals over an open fire pit — which, by the way, had to be fed, too. The extra chores of gathering and splitting wood for meals was my pay for being a rookie.

Most of all, I learned that moving into camp is a major change in outlook and you'd better be out looking all the time.

By the next year, when I joined up with Dexter's crew, I had experience in ordering, cooking, and running the kitchen.

But my water problems took a different turn.

Dexter:

We chose the spot for our remote mining camp with much care, as if we were to live our entire life at the confluence of Maiden Pup and North Fork Harrison Creek.

Earlier miners had left their markers, the oldest being the foundation of a prospector's cabin; the most recent, a ten-year-old Chrysler. It was a perfect location. Plenty of high ground for protection (most years) from the river's tendency to glacier in the spring. The pup creek delivered the crispest, cleanest, sweetest water imaginable, truly an elixir, to within fifty feet of the site we chose to put the cook shack.

We had pre-built a one-room shack that would serve as our kitchen/dining hall/bunkhouse during the winter. A total of eight panels, it fit neatly on our '51 Ford flatbed for transport to the camp site. The loader worked perfectly for unloading and setting the walls, but we had to jury-rig a boom on the bucket to get the needed height or lift to put on the roof.

Now, the issue of water. Have you ever run out of water? Say the power was off for a couple of days because of a storm, and your road was blocked so you couldn't run to the store and buy some bottled water. People who have gone through such perilous times tend to do odd things like fill their bathtub whenever dangerous weather is forecast — and they're not getting ready to take a bath.

Some folks in Alaska live in areas where drilling a well is very expensive or the water is heavily mineralized. Eventually, nearly every Alaskan encounters Water Saving Mode: If it's yellow, let it mellow; if it's brown, flush it down.

For a while, we just hauled the water in five-gallon buckets, which were never far away in case our "improvements" to this simple system failed. We set up a siphon to supply a storage tank placed on

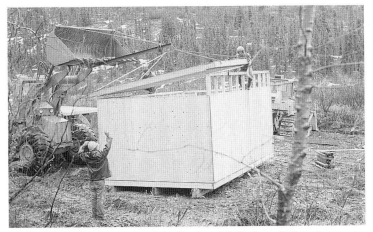

Assembling the cook shack in Spring 1979. It took four hours to rig the "boom" for the five-minute job of setting the roof.

the roof of the cook shack.

Our water "pipeline," designed to keep the storage tank full, was about three hundred feet long. It was a recycler's dream — at least six different kinds and sizes of pipes and hoses were duct taped together resembling an elongated, flexible telescope snaking its way up the valley floor to an itty-bitty dam directing the water into the largest pipe.

In mild weather, this worked beautifully, and the black poly-drum even heated the water somewhat. The downside was fragility. With the least bit of rain, the creek level would rise enough to disrupt our water delivery system. Then the storage tank would run dry and we'd get out the buckets.

After we got settled, Yukon wanted a more reliable water supply. Plus, the storage tank wasn't high enough to provide enough pressure for a shower. We desperately needed a shower. The nearest one was two miles away. But at this time of year, the road, normally in the dry areas of the creek bed, was under ten to twelve feet of glacier ice. As the weather warmed, *our temporary bypass turned from reliable frozen tundra to boot-sucking mud. The crew would go to main camp to get cleaned up, but on the return, they'd get stuck on the "mud road" and wind up dirtier than before their showers.*

By late July, the spring rains were over, and the water level in all the creeks dropped. Again the siphon feed failed. After a clean-up, during the subsequent town run, Yukon pulled me over to look at something in the hardware store. A cute little water pump was the object of her adoration.

"Buy it!" she said.

The pump was an excellent idea. Now we had enough pressure for a shower. This also required the purchase and installation of an in-line, propane-fired hot water heater called a Paloma. Designed for inlet water temperatures of fifty degrees or warmer, the Paloma performed erratically with the water coming in at near freezing, and going out it spurts. So the pleasure of our own shower was often interrupted by blasts of chilly water.

Once the water was in the cook shack, everyone in camp respected the effort that went into getting it there. Conservation and recycling are facts, not just good ideas. The dishwater waits in the sink to be used for washing hands before getting tossed out, or you'd suffer the wrath of Yukon.

Yukon:

With a washing machine right there on site, no longer did I have to travel all the way to Central. (Darn!) Though the old wringer washer was hauled in with no motor, Dexter had hooked it up to a three-horsepower gas engine with a pull start, and it was rigged to fill with a small pump right out of the creek. It sure beat the outfit I had in my first season — our "Bush Maytag" — a

Shoveling cement for the floor of our new shower.

five-gallon bucket and a toilet plunger.

At least once a week I'd remind the crew about laundry day. I'd use the water through three loads (both wash and rinse) then it had to be changed out to fresh.

I had help and thankfully so in Shawn Jones, the ten-year-old son of one of our crewmen. He was well-raised and most of the time he was an eager worker. Sometimes he groused about doing "women's work," like helping me with the laundry or sweeping the cook shack after meals. Though he'd rather have been down in the pit with the men, he learned some valuable lessons at the cook shack.

One day I decided to share a camp secret. I fetched the broom from the mud room and started to sweep while I explained where gold goes when it falls, how deep in the ground it will move, what it takes to catch it. I swept close into the corners, clean out into the middle of the room, filled the dustpan and poured its contents into a gold pan. Then I invited Shawn out to join me at the creek. Getting right down to the "fines" at the pan's bottom, I explained that the "sweep" in camp got to keep that gold. And the laundry crew got to split it! After that, I swear I couldn't find the broom and Shawn never had to be asked to help again.

I'll never forget those happy days on the Harrison. No matter how much hard work was waiting with the next sunrise, I was satisfied down to my core. It's nice to have the fineries of life, but it's also nice to wake up on a crystal clear Sunday morning with the water hauled, the wood chopped, and the laundry done.

I've lived on the banks of a solitary stream, and I've sunbathed on Copacabana Beach in Rio de Janeiro. I'll take the creek, thank you very much. ✿

Fight With a Grizzly
By Dexter Clark

On the day I got thrown by a grizzly bar, we woke to a morning like any other in small mining camps throughout Alaska — five a.m. and time to get started. Yukon and I got up to the early morning light of mid-August. We could see well enough in the cook shack without lighting the propane gas lights. Yukon lit the fire under the coffee she'd made the night before to save on time. Just coffee with Irish Cream for now. Our real breakfast would come later in the morning. With a half-cup still in hand, it was straight down to the pit — as we called our diggings.

Yukon would be operating our four-cubic-yard Terex front-end loader, so she quickly checked the oil levels and made sure she had plenty of fuel. Meanwhile I was making the same pre-work check on the Chevrolet bulldozer, equivalent to a Cat D-8.

The coolness of this morning air was a sign of things to come. The birds were chirping and our mood was a mirror of theirs, encouraged by the frost last week that had knocked down the mosquito population. By five-thirty, both machines were warmed up and ready to dig dirt.

The system we used to get the pay dirt into our sluice box was simple. Through sampling and constant monitoring with the gold pan, we had a good idea of which area we'd be working. I would have already removed the overburden (topsoil and barren gravel) to the side so it could easily be brought back after the cut was finished. So I started pushing up pay dirt into a stockpile close to the dump-bed area of the sluice.

Yukon was ready by now also, so she drove over to the pile I was building, scooped up four yards of pay dirt, and headed up the ramp with a full bucket. This season we were using a prescreen on the sluice to keep out larger rocks and big boulders. The setup was called a grizzly.

I've never wrestled a grizzly bear, but my experience with this piece of mining equipment did me enough harm, you would have thought so. Our grizzly was built with three-inch solid steel bars placed six to eight inches apart at the top and eight to ten inches apart at the bottom. The tapered design kept rocks from sticking and worked pretty good most of the time. Flat, slab-sided bedrock was the exception and was a pain to get out of the bars. Sometimes they'd wedge in and actually break off the bars.

The grizzly rose ten feet above the dump bed, so we built a ramp to get up to it. Yukon had to raise the load of pay twelve feet into the air to clear the edge. On rubber tires, if you're not careful and skilled, you can tip a loader over pretty easily when you have four to five tons of material above your head. But Yukon had made the trip up that ramp thousands of times this summer, and this was just one more load.

The crispness of the approaching fall, the mighty roar of two well-tuned diesel engines, and the knowledge that gold was going in the box all contributed

Heading up the ramp with a load of pay dirt to dump through the grizzly. The large bars screen out the "bull rock" that undoubtedly would choke the sluice box.

to a feeling that all was well in the world. I pushed another twenty tons of rock up into the stockpile, being careful not to drive the forty-ton bulldozer up on the pile and compacting it, which would make it harder for Yukon to load.

A quick look toward the sluice box told me it was time to go push tailings. Whatever goes into the one end of the sluice has to be pushed away from the other. If ignored too long, the rocks will plug the sluice.

Pushing tailings has always been a chore bringing mixed emotions for me. It has to be done, yet there is a certain resentment to pushing rock that doesn't have any gold in it. On the other hand, it's a no-brainer. There's absolutely no pressure on a skilled operator — just push the tailings away from the end of the sluice in a fan shape. The job is so boring that it's possible to catch a few winks on the way up the pile. Now I know it seems impossible that anyone driving around a fifty-ton machine could fall asleep. Think back to when you learned how to drive a car, and the excitement and challenge that kept you alert. Then, after a few years of driving, a little nod here, a little nap there, and you're asleep at the wheel with the best of them. To avoid tragedy, the trick is to keep your ears tuned to the change in the pitch of the diesel engine, when the engine speed goes up, the push is at an end.

By the time I got the tailings all cleaned out, the stockpile needed replenishing. If the loader operator runs out of pay dirt, no gold can be put in the sluice box.

The most important aspect of any mining operation is to make sure there's sufficient gold in the pay dirt. Using the gold pan, testing begins on the surface, and you test-pan again every foot or so as you go deeper. If there is no extra help in camp, this duty is carried out by the dozer operator. That's where speed panning comes in handy. It should take less than five minutes.

Working a cut is an art form unto itself. The material in your cut that is the farthest downstream from the stockpile location is the first dirt pushed up. This blade width is taken out as deeply into the bedrock as you're going to go. The idea is that the pay dirt in front the bulldozer blade is always being pushed over the top of virgin, or unmined, ground. That way if any gold falls out the bottom, eventually maybe even in the next pass, that gold will get caught up in another load.

The resultant mined area, a series of these parallel dozer width cuts, has an unusually smooth and level bottom. That's also nice for the loader operators to have a flat pit floor to work on.

We were close to being done for the day when a large angular slab of bed rock jammed in the bars of the grizzly, causing one of them to break loose and fall into the bull rock pile. That was the sign: We were done sluicing for the day. If we kept going, large rocks certainly would fall through the gap and plug the sluice.

Even though we couldn't mine, our work day was far from over. The grizzly had to be fixed. First thing was to get the service truck with the welder in the back. We pulled it close enough to reach the base of the dump bed. Then we hooked a chain to the bar, which was too heavy for one man to lift.

Yukon was in the loader with the bucket up over the top of the grizzly. We had enough chain hooked to the bucket so we could reach the heavy bar. With the help of the hydraulics, it was easy to get the grizzly bar back into position. The tricky part was to hold it there while it was welded. Did I mention the loader didn't have any brakes?

Yukon was trying to hold everything in place with just the right amount of foot pressure on the accelerator. The bar was in the right position. I had the welding hood on with the stinger in my hand ready to tack weld the brace that held the bar in place.

Everything would have been fine except the hydraulic ram tended to bleed off ever so slightly. Just as I was putting my hood down to weld, the bucket leaked down, the chain lost its grip and that three-hundred-pound bar came sliding down the side of the dump bed. My attempts to hold it up were completely futile. One end caught the inside of my left leg, picking me up off the rock pile and tossing me like I was a rag doll.

My leg was hurting like you wouldn't believe. I couldn't get my pants down quick enough to survey the damage. No blood, no broken bones, just a huge purple bruise that already completely circled my leg.

Yukon was terrified that I'd been killed, but she had to set the loader bucket on the ground, climb down, and cross the sluice box before she could see that I was injured but not seriously.

Yukon argued that I needed to get off that leg,

but I was the only welder in camp. Despite the pain, I insisted we finish the repair job. This time we tack-welded the chain to the bar so there was no encore.

It was a good thing we finished the repair. The next day I couldn't stand on the leg at all. The multi-colored bruise was now from the knee to the hip. It was a full five days before I could crawl up on the dozer and do any meaningful work.

I've never heard of a situation where tissue is scarred without ever breaking the skin, but to this day my left leg has a half moon scar in the shape of that bar.

On the upside, I love to see the look on people's faces whenever I tell them how a grizzly bar threw me thirty feet and that I lived to tell about it. ✿

TRICIA BROWN

Even with regular maintenance, mining machines break down, usually at odd angles or on uneven ground.

Natural Laws
and Unnatural Patience
By Dexter Clark

The first law of mining at any remote site: Get yourself a staging area. In areas of previous mining activity, sometimes a nice flat spot already exists, or an old tailing pile can be leveled to make one. This area is used to park, service, and repair the machinery, so diesel fuel and other petroleum products are also stored here.

If you work machinery, it will break down. Some days I spend more time fixing machines than working them. It is a challenge to anticipate certain problems to avoid being up to the tracks in mud when a weak link breaks. Then you have the added sweat of a temporary fix just to get the machine to the staging area.

About half way through my first season mining, the left side brake on my little track loader suddenly stopped working. I went up and down the creek searching for any information about such a problem. My old buddy, Dave, knew a little bit about similar equipment, but couldn't diagnose the exact problem. His recommendation: Since the only shortcoming of operating the machine in this condition was the inability to make left turns, just make all turns to the right.

This solution worked fine for about ten days, then the other brake also failed. If I couldn't make turns, I couldn't get to the sluice box with the pay dirt. No pay dirt, no payday. I was able to make small turns, enough to park the disabled tractor, by putting rocks in front of first one track, then the other.

It was time for professional help.

I drove into Fairbanks to the local Caterpillar dealer. After explaining my situation to the chain of command, I finally met the head of the repair shop. A quick description of what had occurred was enough for him to declare, "Sounds like the brake bands are broken. How often have you been adjusting the brakes?"

I explained that I had been waiting over a month for a maintenance manual, which I'd ordered from them, so the answer to his question was "What adjustment?"

The shop foreman very patiently pulled from his files the schematic of the tractor's braking system. One look revealed what had happened. The brake band went full circle around the brake drum. By not adjusting out the slack caused by constant wear when turning, I had been flexing these bands much like bending a piece of wire until it eventually breaks.

Now that we knew the problem and its cause, I asked him about having them repair it for me.

"Well, we can order the parts. They'll take about four to five days," he said as he checked his calendar. "Then our field service team could come out and fix it, but they have a full schedule for the next two weeks."

No way could I wait that long to get back in the dirt. My only option was to order the parts and attempt the repair on my own. I was able to get a copy of the drawing that showed how everything fit together and some excellent oral advice on the repair procedure.

This repair job brought me the closest ever to quitting the mining game. The difficulties arose one by one, each bringing me closer to complete frustration. First was the disassembly. With proper tools, the procedure would have been simple, but it involved taking the tractor completely apart. My approach was to use the access panels made especially for getting at the brake bands. The shop manager had warned me that it was extremely difficult, yet possible, to take apart the three-piece brake band and maneuver the pieces out through the little access holes. Once the old ones are out of there, he said, just reverse order of disassembly to put in the new parts.

The entire process took five days and five cases of beer. (Is it coincidence that there are twenty-four hours in a day, twenty-four cans of beer in a case?) Each day, when I was at my limit of patience, one thought pervaded my mind, the only option to fixing the bugger was to quit and go home. So I started drinking the beer, quite possibly with that alternative as the objective. After a couple beers, when things didn't look so bad, I would go back to trying to maneuver both my hands through a hole that barely allowed room for one.

Once the first brake band was successfully out of there, I felt a resurgence in faith: *I can do this.* But the beer remained a part of the program. As for "reverse order of disassembly," the broken bands were easier to get out than the new ones were to get back in.

I fought and fought with that machine, cursing the manufacturer, but especially the engineers. How I wished for an engineer, a mechanic, anybody, to share my misery. Two of the pieces went in easily, but no matter what I tried the third part resisted all my efforts to get it inside the brake housing. Finally on the fourth frustrating afternoon, I had the unwilling part as close as ever, but it wouldn't go any further. I sat back and drank another beer. Then I did something I would have never tried completely sober: I started jumping up and down on the part trying to force it past the brake drum and into its proper place.

The fifth time my two hundred pounds came forcefully down on the piece, it popped past the drum and into the housing. It took the rest of the day to put the pieces together and make a complete circle of the brake band again. Not that easy, but by then I could sense triumph.

The other side went together more quickly, now that I had the jumping technique down pat. The last case of beer went down in pure celebration of my accomplishment, so my first day of mining in more than a week started out with a "banger" of a hangover.

During the repair process I'd learned all about the brake adjustment and became religious about making the necessary adjustments every week. When I finally received my repair manual, the first thing I did was open the book to the section on brake band removal and installation. A clear picture showed a mechanic removing a small section of the brake drum with a chisel allowing room for the new brake band to get past it. I considered a letter to them telling them about another way to do it, but I decided they would never understand the part about the beer.

Some memorable repairs are very expensive lessons. Other times, minor problems are indicators of a impending disaster unless certain steps are taken.

We had a situation like this when a major bearing in the transmission of our largest bulldozer started going bad. A small flake of the self-destructing bearing got caught in the oil valve that controls the tractor's turning mechanism. The result: The Cat would only go in circles. It took us three days to tear the crawler apart and find the sliver of steel causing the problem. A close inspection revealed more bearing pieces but no clues as to the culprit.

Finally, in frustration, we took all the twisted and gnarly little pieces to the mechanics in Fairbanks, and they were able to pinpoint the defective part. It was actually a double bearing, so half of it was hidden from view. It was a good thing we stuck to the plan to fix it right or the entire transmission would have been junk when both sides of that bearing let loose.

Reckless behavior brings its own reward and a lot of equipment suffers the consequences. One very early spring afternoon, after I had spent the day carefully bulldozing huge chunks of glacier ice off our road, I decided to "take the scenic route" back to our staging area. This meant following the creek upstream around the backside of last year's tailings pile. I tried to convince myself I needed to check out the situation over there. As I approached the narrowest spot, the spring run-off was squeezed into a mini-torrent. *No problem*, I thought. I raised the dozer blade a bit higher and prepared to drive back up onto the ice to get around the deepest water. The crawler's tracks bit into the ice first crushing it then climbing safely up on top of it. *That's better,* I thought.

Just as I was almost past the hairy part, the bulldozer began to slide sideways toward the creek that looked more like a river right now. There was nothing I could do to stop the sliding. I dropped the dozer blade with no effect, and I was trying to get the ripper down when we slid off the ice and into the creek.

The water was higher than the tracks, a known danger point, so I immediately raised the entire machine up in the air using the blade in the front, the ripper in the rear, and the machine's powerful hydraulics. When I was clear of the water, I shut off the engine and checked the engine oil to looks for signs of water in the oil. Water will make the oil look milky. This oil looked fine. Maybe I got lucky.

I let the Cat back onto the creek bed and got out of that water as quickly as possible. Again, I shut off the engine and checked the oil, still looked good. I knew right away I had been foolish, but I hoped to have gotten away with it.

The next day, after my partner had been running the Cat for about four hours, he came over and said, "It's starting to run hot, and the oil pressure is dropping."

We knew what that meant, but both of us refused to believe it. We went through all the motions — removed the oil pan and looked at the crankshaft bearings. What should have been perfectly smooth metal bearing surfaces were rough and coarsely gouged. The entire engine was "gunny bagged," needing a complete overhaul.

As I stood up behind the Cat trying to figure how this happened, I noticed a layer of fine sand on the top of the ripper. Only then did it all come together: When the dozer slid into the frigid spring run-off waters, the oil in the crankcase was super-chilled instantly, so instead of a normal situation of having a little crankcase pressure being relieved through a vent tube, a vacuum was formed. The engine had sucked in ever so little of that silt water. There wasn't enough silt in the oil to make it milky-looking, but plenty to ruin that engine in less than five hours.

In this situation the engine was removed from the bulldozer and taken to the equipment dealer's shop in Fairbanks. The repairs cost almost $10,000, but the worst part of it all was the unrecoverable week of mining we missed. A close second was my own realization that this down time was the result of a frivolous action on my part with absolutely no one else to even share the blame. But beating myself up over it wouldn't get the machine working again.

I've found out by now that shifting the blame never works anyway. And being taught through lecture doesn't have the same impact. Let's face it — we are here to make our own mistakes. When we goof up, we open the door to education. Who has ever learned a life-long lesson by doing something right the first time, anyway? ✿

No Fear of Flying
By Dexter Clark

I've always been fascinated with flying. As I boy on the farm, I used to lie on my back in the grass and daydream about being a pilot as I watched the jets flying across the Midwestern sky. Someday, somehow, I'd learn to fly.

My first ride in a jetliner was when I first came to Alaska in the early '70s. This set the stage, in my mind, for an association of flying with Alaska. It seemed a place where dreams could come true. And, in fact, the job I got on the Trans-Alaska Pipeline was more than I'd ever thought it could be. My official title was Advisory Station Operator, which put me in charge of the weather observations that assisted the Bush pilots who flew supplies into the pipeline camps. Although there was never any official authority to control air traffic, it also was part of the job to notify the pilots of any other aircraft in the vicinity. This put me in direct contact with all these pilots via the radio.

With the infusion of cash into my life, I took the first step toward a pilot's license with ground school training. This education was beneficial to my job in many ways, giving me a better understanding of the situations a private or commercial pilot faces in Alaska. Weather observation sites are few and far between, so every shred of information regarding flying conditions was appreciated.

As the Bush pilots became aware of my interest

in flying, another door of opportunity opened. Whenever possible, several pilots would allow me to fly with them on short flights around the area. I was most impressed with helicopters and their ability to hover or even fly backward. My greatest thrill was riding with Vietnam veterans, flying about ten feet above the ground or following a road or river at low altitude. Pilots talked to pilots, and soon all the regulars knew of my intense interest in flying.

The next step was to start the actual flight training to garner the forty hours of dual instruction that was required for private pilots at that time. My four-weeks-on, two-weeks-off job rotation allowed plenty of time for lessons. Familiarity with airplanes and aviation in general contributed to an easy start with a local instructor. We practiced flying out of Phillips Field, which has since been gobbled up by an expressway that runs through Fairbanks. My worst experience was a near mid-air collision. I glimpsed something coming at us from the right side and instinctively pulled back on the yoke, which my instructor told me was obviously the right thing to do.

The rest of that lesson was especially challenging, and by the time we landed safely, I was wringing wet with sweat. As I was putting away the Cessna 150, I was deep in thought, even thinking of giving up. Then I noticed an elderly woman finishing up her pre-flight inspection. When I saw her get into that airplane and fly off, one thought prevailed: *If she can do it, so can I.*

No pilot can ever forget his or her first solo. Mine was unexpected. As the instructor got out of the plane, his advice was, "Don't forget how to land the airplane." Minutes later I was alone in the air, excited and nervous all at once. A dream achieved and a new door opened.

Now, if only I had my own airplane. The pilots I worked with every day became aware of my quest and

Dexter and his true love, a lady in red named "Michelle."

one of them happened to have an airplane for sale. His Maule Lunar Rocket was a real Bush airplane with lots of horsepower and a tail wheel. The name still sends chills up my spine: *Lunar Rocket!*

It seemed to me that my airplane had a personality, so a name was required. The tail number was N9820M which over the radio was shortened up to "20 Mike." I called her Michelle. Sometimes I would go and sit in that plane and just listen to the radio chatter.

There I was working on the pipeline at an airport with this perfectly good airplane sitting in town. Wouldn't it be neat to have that plane right there at work? Rules prevented me from having my private plane at the pipeline camp, but there was an old airport just across the river where I could put it. No sense in flying up empty, so I took orders from friends for alcohol (which was not permitted) to fly in for them.

I left Fairbanks a little later in the evening than I had planned and flew into some unanticipated weather which resulted in my getting disoriented. It was real scary until I spotted a familiar landmark — the Yukon

River. It was late enough in the year, so darkness was falling and I needed to find a place to land. The first airport I spotted was at another pipeline camp, which I turned toward and promptly landed, much to my relief. After sitting in the airplane for about thirty minutes without incident, I decided to go on into camp and call my friends to let them know I was all right. No sooner had I left the plane than Alyeska Pipeline security made a routine airport check and discovered what they assumed to be a shipment of bootleg alcohol. They confiscated the entire load, not believing my story that it was all my own stuff. The biggest problem with the entire episode was that I was supposed to be on duty during this time. No question about it, I was out of a job. At first light, I flew back to Fairbanks to see what I could salvage.

It took several months to get reimbursed for the booze and to get my job back.

My pipeline job had provided me with enough money to get started in another adventure — gold mining. And the miners I'd become involved with were saying they could use a little air support since their mine was more than a hundred miles from Fairbanks. Over the road, which was under reconstruction at the time, a town trip could take four hours one-way. In the air this was reduced to forty-five minutes.

At first the closest place to land was on that same road about ten miles from camp. I would "buzz" the cabins and someone would drive out to pick me up along with whatever supplies I'd brought.

The building of an airstrip became a priority. A disgruntled investor in another mine offered the use of his outfit's D-9 Cat. The only drawback was he wasn't sure exactly where the Cat was. If I would help him find the dozer, we could use it to build our airport. He had a general idea where to look, so we went up in the plane together and within a couple hours spotted our objective and plotted a route to retrieve it. The twenty-mile "walk" of that bulldozer took two days, but it only took a day to rough in a thousand-foot runway. Harrison Creek International Airport came into being.

My first trip into that airstrip I brought a rare treat for the miners — fresh pizza, half-baked and oven-ready. According to the entire crew, the arduous airport building effort was already worth it. Even Sam, the main miner, was convinced. He'd once said he would never fly in anything he could put his fist through (most Bush planes are fabric-covered).

One spring when there was still lots of snow on the ground, Sam and his crew decided to head out to the mine and get the remaining gold out of the sluice box. To this day, the rest of that crew maintains Sam was trying to get away from creditors, and being out on the creek was the ideal place.

Anyway, they left Fairbanks on three snowmachines with two sleds full of supplies. I was out of town at the time, but upon my return I got a call from the office in town. Sam and the boys hadn't been heard from in several days. Would I go out with the plane and check on them?

The next morning I headed north. I followed the road in case they had had problems on the way. No sign of them on the main road, but shortly after turning to follow the trail into the mine, I spotted smoke from the chimney of an old cabin. As I circled around, Sam came out of the cabin and started jumping up and down like a little kid at Christmas. I landed on the main road, which was snow-covered and rutted by snowmachine tracks. This presented no problem since Michelle was wearing her skis. I was not far from the plane when Sam came huffing up the trail on snowshoes. Boy, was he glad to see me and that airplane! He was ready to get out of there. They had already blown the engines on two of the sno-gos and they hadn't gotten within five miles of their destination. I took him back to town and returned with gas, spark plugs and other supplies and helped the crew get into camp and ultimately down to the sluice. It took us five days to get five ounces of gold out of there. Not really worth the effort.

Later that spring, Ron Lipke was hauling us a load of mining equipment with a semi-tractor trailer when the tractor broke down. Lipke, a.k.a. Big Lip, needed to be flown to town to get parts. As he was supposed to be picking up another load later that afternoon for some other miners, we decided we should notify them of the problem. Otherwise, they'd be sitting and waiting for two days. *We'll just drop them a note from the airplane on the way into town.*

Sam's brother, Rollie, prepared an elaborate airdrop parcel made from an empty chewing tobacco canister. The note explaining the situation was rolled up inside the canister, and streamers of surveyors flagging were taped to the outside for tracking ease in case the package was a little off target. The final attachment was a handkerchief parachute that Rollie insisted was necessary.

Big Lip and I started for town with him giving directions as to where he was supposed to meet the Nelson Boys. We spotted their pick-up truck in a clearing near the top of a hill and circled around to get their attention. I wagged the wings and they waved back. We had contact.

This would be my first attempt at an aerial delivery, so I was anxious to get it on target. There were so many factors involved: the speed of the airplane, the size of the clearing, and the potential for wind carrying our message into the trees. I slowed the plane down as much as was safe and we made our approach.

I slid open the cockpit window and got the package ready for tossing. We came in over the clearing, low and slow. *Now!* I thought and pitched the canister out and away from the plane. I glanced back to check our flight path, and we were clear. *Time to close the window, but wait, something's on the wing strut.*

It was amazing. The parachute had gone around one side of the strut and the canister around the other. The parachute was open, catching enough air to balance the weight of the package. How long would it hang there? By now, we were well away from the drop zone. If the note fell off, there would be no way the Nelsons would find it. We did not have the resources to make another note. We needed to get that one back.

I yelled to Big Lip, "Here, fly the airplane!" and started to crawl out the window to retrieve the flapping package. Just my upper body was out of the cockpit, and it only took about ten seconds to get back in with the parcel in hand. Since my newly appointed co-pilot had never flown an airplane before, we'd lost a lot of altitude. I pulled the yoke back just in time to clear another ridge that was looming.

"Don't you *ever* leave the airplane with me in it again!" were the first words the obviously shaken truck driver was able to get out.

His statement required no response. With the plane back in my control, we came back to the clearing again. This time I made sure that the canister went straight down from the plane.

It was several months before we found out that the second drop was a success. With the parachute open and the bright surveyor's flagging marking its descent, the canister with its crucial note inside came down just at the edge of the clearing. It was my first and last air drop, all in the course of a regular day of gold mining.

On another occasion after supper, I'd gone back to the pit to work on the sluice box, when two of the guys from the main camp crew came rushing up in their "crummy," or crew-haul pickup. Obviously very excited, they both tried to talk at the same time. Something about an accident, a couple kids hurt, one's throwing up blood, could I fly them to town?

I left my tools right there, jumped in the truck with them, and began to sort out the story as we raced toward the airstrip where I kept the plane. Chris and Richard, both barely teen-agers, had been riding their motorbikes up and down the creek all afternoon. They'd split up for a while, then went looking for each other. They met, head-on, at one of the many blind corners in the creek road. Glen, the cook, had gotten worried because he hadn't seen the boys for a while so he went looking for them. He had found them lying in the road- way with the smashed bikes beside them.

When we arrived at the plane, we were met by the worried families who had both boys, one unconscious, the other semi-alert, ready for the flight to town. I had already arranged for my escorts to put more fuel in the plane when I found out that Dick, the father of the more seriously injured Richard, wanted to stay with his son. As soon as I heard that, I stopped the airplane refueling effort to keep the take-off weight at a minimum.

We took out the back seat so we could lie Richard out flat. His dad got in beside him. Chris needed a lot of help before he was situated in the right front seat. Exuding a courage I really didn't feel, I taxied to the far- thest, usable, downwind part of the runway and turned the plane around.

Before revving the engine, I turned and asked Dick, "You guys ready back there?"

He nodded and if there was an oral answer it was

lost in the roar as I applied full power to the 210-horse-power engine still holding the plane back with the brakes. With his assent, I released the brakes and Michelle jumped forward, eager to get into the air. As we started bouncing down the runway that I prayed we be long enough, I shouted into the back seat to Dick. "Could you lean forward a bit?" Once his body weight was shifted from the aft bulkhead to behind the front seats, the tail wheel came off the ground, three seconds later we were in the air headed for the hospital.

As soon as we had cleared the mountains, I radioed ahead to Fairbanks to let them know we had injured passengers requiring an ambulance. The flight was uneventful other than Chris moaning as he drifted in and out of consciousness. This changed when we got closer to the airport where the tower operators wanted as much information as possible. They also directed me to land on the black-topped main runway, a first for me. Our landing was a little wobbly probably because of the unfamiliar pavement under the wheels.

The kids were hustled off to the hospital in the waiting ambulance. I stood alone on the tarmac for a minute, digesting what had happened. Then I hopped back into the plane, got clearance from the tower, and took off only to land five minutes later at the smaller airport where most of the private pilots kept their Bush planes.

First thing the next morning, I went over to the hospital. Chris had been treated and released. Richard had a broken collarbone, but was in good condition. The blood that everyone thought he was throwing up turned out to be blueberries he'd been eating that afternoon. What had felt like a life-and-death situation the night before was now just another couple of youngsters learning the hazards of growing up at a gold mine.

Flying back to the mine by myself, I realized how important it was to have good neighbors. This time, I had been the one to come to their aid. Next time, who knows? It could be me relying on them, simply for a part to fix a machine, or for their help in a truly life-or-death situation. I was just glad that Michelle and I were there.

My last great airplane adventure began with a routine flight over the mine in the spring to check on the glacier situation near our camp. It was an unusual year in that the glaciers were growing earlier and faster than we had ever seen. One look was all that was needed to see that the equipment we had left high and dry in the fall was now locked in the growing Arctic ice.

The loader was in the worst situation, with glacier ice already nearing the engine. Some sort of rescue operation was needed or we would have an expensive repair bill.

Since the runway was buried under an uneven sheet of ice that ranged anywhere from ten to twenty feet thick, we needed an alternate place to land.

An aerial survey of the area revealed that the closest place to land safely in the snow with a ski-equipped plane was the top of Harrison Summit. We flew back to town and began preparations immediately for a return trip with some supplies and gear for the camp.

It looked like the easiest way to get from the summit down to main camp was to cross-country ski. Once we made it, we'd try to get an old snowmachine going to take us two more miles downstream to our camp. We planned for contingencies such as an overnight stay or problems getting machines to start, so the airplane was fully loaded when we left town.

The landing went smoothly, or at least it was a lot less memorable than the ski trip down the mountain. I broke trail most of the way because my skis were an extra-wide military surplus model made for deep, untracked snow. Yukon fought her way down the mountain on her much narrower commercial variety of skis. The air turned blue as the thin boards strapped to her feet repeatedly threw her into the snow banks.

When we finally got to the cluster of cabins at the base of the summit, she was ready to start a fire, but not so much to warm up. We were quite warm from the exertion. She just wanted to burn those skis on the spot.

With the help of a little ether, the old reliable snowmachine came alive. We hooked up a sled for Yukon and headed down the creek, picking our way over the glaciers when necessary, returning to the road when possible. We were within sight of our camp when I felt the load on the snowmachine evaporate. I turned around in time to see the tongue of the sled dig deeply into the snow on the trail. The sled had stopped abruptly, but Yukon kept on going, headfirst into a big snow drift. Since there was nothing to be gained by stopping, I continued the hundred yards or so to the camp. With a wide circle I headed back to help her out of the snow. To this day, she feels like I left her in a time of need when all I wanted to do was get turned around.

Much to our surprise, both of the machines started right up and we got them out of the threatening ice to higher ground. We could look for hidden damage later. It seemed we might get out the same day. That was a relief because you never know what the weather is going to do to your plans. We could be snowed in for days.

With our main objective achieved, we headed back to main camp. Yukon got to build that fire she wanted so badly as I took the sno-go up the summit to break a trail back to the airplane.

I reached the base of the summit without incident, but when I tried going up the mountain, the snowmachine floundered in the deep snow and stopped. The only thing to do was get turned around, head back down the mountain to a solid spot at the bottom and race back up along the partially packed portion of the trail. Each round-trip would extend the trail up the mountain, most times only a few hundred feet. So went the rest of the afternoon, with one break to refuel. When I finally made it to the plane, there was only about an hour of daylight left.

I went back to the camp to discuss options with Yukon. Although I was really tired from fighting the trail up the summit, neither of us had any desire to spend the night and risk tomorrow's weather. "Let's go for it," we agreed.

Since we had never hauled any supplies down from the summit other than the skis on our feet, we doubled up on the snowmachine and headed for the top.

At the plane, we put the sno-go out of the way and clamored into the cockpit. The impending darkness meant we would just be flying over to the Hot Springs, less than a ten-minute flight. The airplane engine's roar broke the stillness of the late afternoon. "You ready? This could get bumpy," I warned Yukon.

I didn't realize how bumpy. As soon as we started moving across the snow field, the airplane started losing the ground track left when we flew in. *Probably should have packed a better runway with the snowmachine*, I thought briefly. Once the tail wheel was out of the snow, we began to pick up speed, although not in the direction intended. I tried to look ahead for problems in our ground track, but there was only a blinding field of whiteness without relief. The airspeed indicator said we should be in the air by now.

Just as the skis broke the bond with the earth, a large snow drift loomed in our path. I pulled up, hoping once we got over the drift, a nose-down attitude would recover our airspeed and we'd be out of there. "Hang on!" I yelled at Yukon.

I heard a thump, then silence, as the plane settled

back into the snow, slid for a few seconds, and then came to rest.

The load behind us had shifted somewhat. As the pilot's door creaked open, a untouched bottle of whiskey came over my shoulder, fell into the snow and started skittering away. With one smooth move, I captured that bottle, spun the cap off, and took a long deep swig. Then I handed it to Yukon. "Here you go. We just survived a plane crash."

When we got out of the plane, the damage became more visible, accompanied by a realization of how close a call it had been.

Yukon brought a little levity to our situation by proclaiming, as she stood by the twisted propeller: "If nothing else gets down off this mountain, I want the prop. We are now the proud owners of an Alaskan Longhorn, full-curl."

We gathered up supplies enough for a night in the camp that we'd just left, and reluctantly, we turned our backs on the downed bird. That night was almost surreal. I kept hoping that the crash had been a dream.

The next morning we hooked up the sled again, drove effortlessly up the mountain over the now-hard trail, unloaded all the gear from the plane and headed for Central. Going down the other side was no picnic. The wind-blown snowdrifts over the road eliminating the once-flat surface. To stay aboard the sled, Yukon spent most of time leaning into the mountain.

Nearly five hours later, we stumbled into the first sign of civilization, the Central Lodge. We announced our arrival with an order for a couple drinks, better make them a double, we just crashed our plane.

"So we can call off the search?" questioned the bartender.

"What search? We weren't on any flight plan. No one else knows we crashed." Only then did we recall the

TRICIA BROWN

We made it with our skins intact, but the prop didn't fare as well. Yukon calls it my "Alaskan Longhorn, full-curl"!

unusual amount of air traffic we'd seen that morning.

It turned out another small plane had crashed at about the same time we had. When they found that one, it was burned, nose to tail. No survivors.

Yukon called her Dad in Fairbanks to let him know what had happened. "Do you have all your fingers and toes?" he asked her.

"Yes."

"Then tell Dexter it was a good landing."

I proceeded to get as drunk as I've ever been. Passed out and awoke again hoping this had all been a dream. We took the mail plane home that afternoon. As we flew over Michelle lying crippled on that mountain top, our pilot looked down and said, "What an odd spot to park an airplane."

The salvage operation was easy. We just had to wait for the snow to melt. Once the road was open, we took her wings off and loaded her on a flat bed for her last journey to Fairbanks.

I have not piloted a plane since that day, but it hasn't been out of fear. It's only because of finances.

I will fly again. ✿

AL GRILLO

Who can figure what goes on in the mind of a moose?

The Wild Ones

Of Moose and Men
By Dexter Clark

There is a cardinal rule in our mining camp: You shoot it, you eat it. One time a miner working with us wanted to shoot a raven. All the arguments about the raven's status as a sacred bird in the Alaska Native cultures were to no avail. He didn't even care that it was protected by federal law under the Migratory Species Act. He was going to shoot him a raven. Finally, when we told him that if he shot it, he would be eating it, he grumbled something, but he never talked about shooting a raven again.

Most wild animals steer clear of mining camps. Ravens are an exception. They track man and his rubbish all over the Arctic. However, moose and caribou had established trails following the creeks in this country long before men sought gold in the same valleys. A confrontation is inevitable, and the next moose that gets shot for trespassing won't be the first.

One year, my sister Georgia was spending part of her summer at the mine, helping with the cooking and camp chores. Naturally, she brought along her five-year-old son, Chris. Since she felt it was safer for both of them to remain near camp, I was surprised when she showed up in the cut one day near noon. She needed some help. It seems she had spent the entire morning trying to chase a cow moose away from the camp.

What could be the problem with that moose? I went with her back to the camp, and it wasn't five minutes before a 1,200-pound cow moose came crashing through the brush to stand at the edge of camp, bellowing. Just then, little Chris came out of the cook shack to see what was going on. Boy, was he surprised to see this big old moose start coming toward him. He tried to run back into the cook shack, but the cow had placed herself between Chris and the building, and kept bellowing.

It started to make sense when we saw the cow's udder. It was bloated, terribly swollen. She had somehow recently lost her calf and was going to adopt this human as her baby. We got Chris to safety and the moose retreated to the edge of the clearing. Then she began bellowing again. We tried several times to chase her off, but she wasn't leaving. We decided to go back to work and see what happened.

Less than an hour later, Georgia came back to the pit and again demanded we do something about that cow. She was in fear for her son as well as herself. We further decided that the cow was in a lot of misery, could possibly get mastitis and besides, we could use some camp meat. Even though we were justified in taking the cow moose because she was "a threat to life or property," we dealt with the carcass as though we had poached it.

The first part of this is not pretty, because to quarter a moose quickly, the best and fastest method is to use a chain saw. Some poachers use a special chain saw that has never cut any wood. They will use vegetable oil to lubricate the chain and bar. I hear it works great.

After the carcass was quartered, we cleaned all the blood and hair off of the chain saw by cutting into the glacier ice near the camp. A neighboring miner advised us to cool the meat quickly by putting the entire moose quarter into the cold, clear water of the stream. We tried this trick in an appropriate pool.

Definitely not the way to take care of a moose. We shared the meat around the valley including those who'd given us this suggestion, *especially* those who'd given us the suggestion. The meat was not actually bad, but there was a distinct blood flavor that we surmised was from not letting the meat hang properly.

On the other hand, if we'd hung the meat, the summer air was so warm that the meat would have gone completely bad. We cooked the moose in stews and, with enough spices, you couldn't tell the meat had been mishandled. Miners are always resourceful, and new ways of cooking were invented just so the meat wouldn't be wasted.

Every time we sat down to a dinner of well-seasoned moose, the story of the moose's bizarre behavior had to be reviewed. Everyone agreed that she intended to adopt our young nephew, but no one had ever heard of anything like this happening before. As we discussed her actions in human terms of motives and wants, we began to personify her, somewhat regretting the necessity to end her misery.

Upon reflection, I now believe that another factor may have influenced the strange flavor we tasted in that moose meat. It came together months later when we were having dinner at a local restaurant, when the taste of this moose was only a memory. Yukon was in the process of explaining to me why the chef puts food on the plate that you're not supposed to eat. I think she used the word "presentation." I confess that my other ear was listening in on a conversation at the next table. They were talking about going moose hunting. I almost asked them if they'd ever heard of a moose hunting a human. Better just eat my dinner and not reveal I'd be eavesdropping.

But now I was thinking about that old cow moose again. Maybe we should have tried putting parsley sprigs and orange slices on the plate, too. Then I realized that every meal she'd provided did come with some garnish — the story of her human-like maternal instincts.

I recalled the haunting image of a mother who'd had lost her child and was so miserable that she faced certain death to try and replace him. Could it be that we, a bunch of hard-core miners, had a shared a taste of her sorrow? ✿

Meeting Utah
By Yukon Yonda

In Alaska, there are plenty of stories about contact between wolves and humans. Some are hunts, some just chance meetings in the Bush. Others are the scientific study of the species over of long period of time. I'd like to tell you about meeting Utah.

My first year in Alaska passed very quickly. I spent it mostly in wide-eyed wonderment, feeling my way around the town. Early on I was getting advice from the sourdoughs on where to settle, what I'd need for the seasons. I had decided on a cabin with no water but with electricity. I found such a place in Ester, just eight short miles southwest of Fairbanks.

Ester is a small community, boasting the widest variety of a hundred fifty people that could be found and deliberately assembled. They were gold miners, artists, carpenters, jewelry makers, welders, heavy-equipment operators, sculptors, teachers, and writers. As in the past, Ester is still producing gold and the Ester-ites still claim "republic" as the status of their small community.

In the mid-1970s, Ester had two saloons: the Malemute Saloon of the historical Cripple Creek diggings, and The Red Garter, where I worked. It was a pretty lively place, and open from May to early October if the weather held. The saloon had originally been built into the hill behind it — that way, the old-timers saved on heat and refrigeration. Over the years, the building had served for different businesses. It had once been the general store and post office. As a saloon, it had seen add-ons a couple of times, and now had sawdust for the floor with an open rafter ceiling.

By 1976, the Red Garter was noticeably leaning away from the hill. Rusty Huerlin, a well-known Alaskan artist and long-time Ester resident, told me not to worry: "Ah, she started that leaning about thirty years ago," he said. The Garter clearly didn't have much longer to live, but still it served the community residents as a place to gather, relax with a game of pool, meet a neighbor, or blow off a little steam on a Saturday night with "JoAnne and Monte" singing our favorite tunes. I loved working at the Garter.

One day while I was on my way to open the saloon, I decided to stop at the Malemute just down the road, to visit the bartenders and staff at the Cripple Creek Hotel. This complex was steeped in local color and history. It had served the mining community for decades and had recently focused its trade on the ever-growing visitor industry. What better place to sample a taste of the present and past Alaska?

The Malemute Saloon also was an old wooden structure with a wide veranda-style porch and swinging doors as its entrance. Inside, it was like stepping back into the middle of the nineteenth century, with the floor covered by peanut shells, the ceiling wrapped in burlap bunting. Artifacts of times past covered the walls, and a huge wheel of Cheddar cheese sat open on the bar.

At the back was a stage where old vaudevillians would hold proud, and where hours of Robert Service poetry was shared with local and visitor alike. To the left was an immense, very ornate mahogany sideboard, with the bar directly in front of it. The bar was the same rich dark wood with a leaning rail attached on top and a foot rest at its base.

A couple of locals, there early, waved me in and offered a refreshment. I accepted and stepped inside. One of the locals was working at the new volunteer fire department and I asked how that was going. We visited for about ten minutes when I noticed, sticking out of the open end of the bar, the back half of a wolf.

My first reaction was to take a good grip of the handrail and stand very still. Slowly I turned to Jim and spoke softly:

"Uh, is that a real wolf at the end of the bar!?"

Jim laughed and said, "Sure, that's Utah!" He proceeded to call him over.

The animal backed up to see who had called, turned, and loped a dozen steps over to us. Jim patted him on the head, asked him to sit, and introduced him.

He was magnificent! The color of his eyes was a mixture of browns with flecks of gold throughout. His thick fur was mostly black, with brown and tan mixed throughout his markings. He was the size of a Great Dane, yet there was something delicate to his bone structure. Sitting, his head was at my waist. A sense of raw power surrounded him. I offered my hand to share my scent and got a little closer.

"Does someone local own him?" I asked Jim.

Jim kind of laughed, "Own?" and shared with me Utah's arrival in Ester.

It seems, as a pup living on the edges of Ester, Utah had come into one of the mining camps several times. They'd fed him scraps and treated him well. As the pup grew friendlier, worried miners put a bandanna on his neck as some sort of "domestication flag."

"He doesn't go to just anyone," Jim said. "For some reason, he decides to be friendly with certain people and shows up, spends some time, then lopes on off."

Utah had taken a liking to a couple of folks in that camp. As he got older, his pick of people enlarged until he had developed a route through town when he visited. This just happened to be one of those occasions.

I stepped next to him, squatted down and had the delicious experience of being eye-to-eye with the legend of the forest. I stayed awhile longer, petting and talking to Utah until I had to leave.

Walking down the dirt road that runs the two-block length of "beautiful downtown Ester," I realized how lucky I was to actually touch a live adult wolf, but if I didn't get a move-on, I'd be late opening the Red Garter.

I stepped into the cool darkness and left the door open to add needed light. I headed toward the back of the building and stepped into my work area. The bar was long and narrow with the service island located at the end toward the center of the building. My work area was sunken into the floor, so when people were sitting at the bar, I was eye-level with the customer.

At the far end, I started to fill the sinks with hot water, soap, and in the rinse water, bleach. With my mind on the chores at hand, I was enjoying this quiet time of preparation knowing that in a couple of hours the place would be filled to the brim and then some.

Suddenly a chilling sensation of danger came over me. I stopped and turned slowly to see if someone was in the building with me. Instead, there at the far end of the bar sat Utah. He was sitting there soundlessly, for how long, I don't know. His ears were laid back flat against his skull. His eyes were level and staring directly at me. Seconds passed. For some reason I got the distinct impression he was smiling. I smiled back at him and broke the silence: "Utah, you just scared the starch out of me!"

With that he rose to his full height, wiggled like a puppy that had just gotten away with something, and trotted over to me throwing his massive head as if to say, "Yeah, I know!"

That visit was the beginning of a long relationship with a most unusual friend. Sometimes Utah would meet me on the trail back from the town well when I was hauling water for the cabin. Or he would come to the cabin and sit out front. Usually I'd notice when he was there. But on many occasions, if I was busy inside, he would "call" me out. I loved it when he'd come inside with me, but the cabin was small and one wolf would fill it up.

Utah's visits were more frequent in the spring and summer. In the warmer weather, he'd join me as I sat next to a tree. Side by side, we enjoyed the sun and the bright days. I'd watch while he'd play with some of the local dogs, and if there were puppies around, Utah would take on the image of an old uncle doling out his wisdom and tolerating foolishness.

After a couple of years, I moved away from Ester, and the Red Garter finally was torn down. To keep up on the news in Ester, whenever I was in town, I'd stop in at the Malamute. I could count on Joel, the bartender, to have the latest. Even though the Malamute was closed in the winters, he stayed on the property year-round as watchman. One day, I asked what Utah had been up to lately. Joel's face grew serious.

"I was making my rounds one day, when I found Utah lying out there in the snow in the parking lot," Joel said, shaking his head. "I didn't know what was wrong with him, but I went and got a blanket. I wrapped him up and carried him to my cabin."

Joel went on with his grim story: "Once inside,

I set Utah near the barrel stove and ran my hands over him, looking for some kind of wound. Nothing."

Joel said he'd figured Utah was all right, that he just needed a rest. He said Utah drank some water, ate a little, then went to sleep. He went back out to finish his rounds, came back to the cabin, checked Utah again, banked the stove for the night, and went to bed.

"Come morning," Joel continued, "when I woke up, I called to Utah, but he didn't lift his head. That's when I went over and found him dead. His bedding was soaked with blood, and when I turned him over I found the entrance wound of the bullet that killed him."

I was stunned. Unbelievable. Our conversation turned to the same, unanswered questions Joel had asked himself since that day: *Who could have shot him? Why, when everyone knew he was tame?*

"What a shame! What a terrible loss!" I thought over and over. I assured Joel that he'd done what was expected of a friend — he'd tried to help.

That afternoon, the drive from Ester back to Fairbanks was long, quiet, and sad. Someone had just pulled a trigger. A simple motion, like when Utah smiled. ✿

TRICIA BROWN

In the summer of '82, I gathered the animals for a family photo. Clockwise, from top: Duffy, Piper, Ernie, and Bountiful.

Fur Better or Worse

A Mining Type Dog
By Yukon Yonda

The folks at the Fairbanks North Star Borough animal shelter do a good job tending to the adoptions of extra puppies in litters, sled dogs past their prime, strays, and this mongrel peering out at me.

I'd been longing for a dog. I'd been raised around various pets my whole life, and had missed the companionship of a canine sidekick for many years. Five of those years were spent in an apartment in Chicago where I didn't think it was fair for a dog to live as cooped-up as I.

With my birthday coming in a couple of months, I figured this would be my present to me. I headed straight for the puppy pen. There they were, all facing me. An entire pen full of squirming, yipping, whining, piddling with excitement, promises of loyalty and good times to come.

Then I noticed one small dog beneath the wiggling pack. Not a puppy but still young, and definitely growling as he looked up and out at me.

Instantly he won the competition. I always will focus immediate attention on a growling dog. Reaching over the side, I picked him up and brought him eye to eye, saying, "Hey! Don't be 'growly' at me. I can bust you out of here, Bud."

His eyes pleaded with me in no uncertain terms: *Get me out of here!* I called over an attendant, who told me the former owners were moving to the Lower 48. Also, records showed that in two days he'd take his last short walk. Rules are rules, and after a set amount of days the animals have to be destroyed.

He was a stoic little guy, about five months old. He appeared to be a cross between of a couple kinds of terriers and would not be a large animal. Short, thick, coarse kind of fur, dark guard-hairs with a tan under-coat. There's really no way to describe petting him. The first time I did, I had to look at my hand because I never felt fur quite like that. It was the terrier cross that probably won me over. There's a determined streak in that breed, and since I had one of those, too, I thought we ought to partner up!

He had borne the indignity of the puppy pen to a full measure but he wasn't much excited at his release either. As a matter of fact, it took a full year for him to wag his tail at me. On this day, fifty dollars later, he was heading to a new home in Ester, with a new partner and a new name: Duffy.

My 30.06, backpack, guitar, and Duffy were what was first seen of me wading the creeks when I started mining in the Circle District.

He was very critical regarding meeting new people and took two years to approve of Dexter. I don't know a single detail regarding the "deal" they eventually struck. That was never my business, and Dexter hadn't a clue. I just came downstairs one day to find Duffy sitting on Dexter's lap like it was something he'd been doing for years.

Once he approved his association with someone, he would conduct full and complete conversations through either simple body language or a very throaty verbiage while maintaining eye contact. Some claimed

My first mining partner. In no time at all, Duffy made himself useful as a pint-sized guard dog.

he was telepathic and could simply throw his thoughts into your brain, as if he were the ventriloquist and you were the dummy. He gathered fans wherever he went.

If Dexter and I weren't home when my sister came out to the house, she'd kidnap the dog, leaving a note that Duffy was spending the night. She called him her "hairy nephew." My brother regularly left notes on the front door that read "Took Duffy fishing" or "Took Duffy skinny-dipping."

Dexter and I had been working together for about a year when he heard a longtime friend and his wife were leaving Alaska. He got a message to them that we should try and get together before they left. A couple of days later they called with a dinner invitation. They were looking forward to a long visit and to tell us about their plans.

The temperature was twenty-five below on the night of our visit, so we tucked everything in, patted

Duffy on the head, and headed out for Chena Hot Springs Road. Their cabin was located a few miles from the main road. Because of traffic from both snowmachiners and dog teams, the trail was well-packed and easy-going. Off we trudged, under layers of warm clothes, leaving clouds of steam from our breath as we traveled. The night was brightly lit by the moon, and we were looking forward to touching bases with friends.

About half-way down the lane to the cabin, one of the most beautiful animals I'd ever seen came out on the trail. She greeted us with a bark and joined us as we called to the cabin from the trail. She was a large dog with bright, intelligent eyes set in a black and white face. Her powerful body was covered with long fur and her softly curved tail bounced as she walked ahead of us. She seemed to be a malemute but with a strong cross of some other very large breed. We found out later it was Great Pyrenees. She'd also recently whelped a litter of puppies. Her name was Bountiful, or Bounty for short.

Dexter and I arrived at the cabin with a grand welcome! Stepping out of the Arctic evening into a kitchen warmed by a wood cookstove, we were enveloped by steam. Bounty headed straight for the box next to the stove to tend her babies, and we shared with our host all the greetings old friends bring to each other. Dinner was bubbling on the stove; the table was laden like it was Thanksgiving.

Our hosts were set to leave in the next few days, but they still had a few things to do before departure. One job was to deal with Bounty and her litter of puppies in the box. If homes could not be found, the little family would have to go to the animal shelter. The puppies, of course, would be no problem but adults weren't adopted so easily. I thought of Duffy and his adoption. I also thought, "No! Don't need another dog, especially one this large!"

The entire evening was just plain fun. Hearing their plans for living Outside and seeing how excited they were about this move was infectious. And, as though she'd adopted me as a new best friend, Bountiful stayed by my side through the entire evening except, of course, when her puppies needed her. Sometime that evening, my resolve caved in. I wanted this dog.

Our conversation moved to times past. Coming into this country, times spent working on the pipeline, and Dexter's venture into the mining game. As the night grew to a close, we promised to drive our friends to the airport and, yes, if homes were found for all the puppies, we'd add Bountiful to our pack.

Heading home, Dexter and I talked about Duffy and how he would accept another dog. We knew one thing that was in our favor: This addition was a female. We came home telling Duffy we'd found him a girl-friend — four times his size, but still, a girlfriend. As it turned out, Duffy and Bountiful would be a love story that would rival any Disney movie.

When Duffy was introduced to Bounty, it was as if he'd been "pole-axed"! Life could now begin. By day, he went everywhere she went. And when they were in the house for the night, he'd sit off to her side and gaze at her in blind adoration. Duffy and Bounty became a constant either in camp, out hunting, or at home. In gaining another house pet, it appeared I had lost my original mining partner.

One early spring, Bounty came into her cycle and disappeared. I wasn't too alarmed though. Whenever she was in heat, she'd usually take off instead of waiting for the local males to come around. She'd be gone for three or four days, then come home, pregnant, of course, and sleep for three days.

But this time she was overdue coming home. I started calling for her whenever I went outside to feed our meat rabbits or take care of some other chore. I listened for her return call but heard nothing. By the third day, I was getting worried, and I noticed that Duffy was behaving strangely, like he could hear something I couldn't.

Duffy's attention was focused across the road, which like our property on this side of the road, is nothing but forest and foothills. Taking Duffy's clue, I returned to the house to put on more clothes and warmer shoes. I told Dexter that I believed Duffy was on to something, and headed out the door.

"Find Bountiful! Where's Bountiful?!" I said to Duffy. There was an urgency in my voice. Wasting no time, he turned and headed out the driveway, then crossed the highway. Next to our mailbox, he started out on a trail toward the back wall of the valley.

The snow was very deep in places, and Duffy skirted those spots as if he knew just where to go. We'd traveled about a quarter-mile when I tried calling again. This time I heard her, a faint bark in the distance. But which direction? Each time I called, she barked back. I tried to sound her down but I couldn't get a fix on the direction. We were in a section of the valley where the sound bounced all around. Looking to Duffy to steer me, we traveled another quarter-mile. He stopped at the top of a set of tailing piles and just over the rim, down in the gully was my Bountiful. Thank God! I was relieved, and was she ever glad to see me!

Duffy bounded over to her and sat quietly. That's when I saw the trap attached to her foot. In efforts to extract herself, she had caused the trap to freeze over from her breath. The foot wasn't severed, but it certainly was frozen. Lacking tools to bust her out, I turned to Duffy and told him to stay with her. He seemed to sit at attention. I then started for home to get Dexter and help.

"She's been lucky," I thought as I headed back. The weather had been fairly mild the last few nights, and she'd been able to eat snow to keep from dehydrating. The going was a little easier as I followed the same trail that Duffy and I had taken. I trotted home as fast as I could, imagining how upset Bounty must be to see me turn around and leave her there. By the time I was within earshot of the house, I was sobbing and out of breath.

"Dexter! We found her!" I yelled as I ran down the driveway. He met me on the porch and my words poured out with my tears: "She's about a half-mile from here, across the valley, and her foot's stuck in an old trap. It's frozen up. I couldn't get her out."

We decided Dexter would head back to the dogs and I would call our vet for advice on the care of a frozen foot.

In short order, Bountiful, Duffy, and Dexter came back down the driveway. The vet had suggested we drive into town so he could begin the thawing process. While Dexter started the truck to warm it up, Bountiful, happy to be home, seemed unaffected —

After a week of trying to save Bounty's frozen foot, we knew it was beyond hope. It had to come off.

except for the sound of her stride. Our floor is concrete, and as she walked there was a clicking of her nails and then a "thump" from her rock-hard front foot. She had no trouble walking, she was just really noisy when she did. Duffy, even more attentive than usual, stayed right by her side.

In one short week we knew the foot would have to come off. Both Dexter and I wondered how this would affect our big mama dog. However, other than the occasional trip-up when she seemed to forget the foot was gone (*was that embarrassment on her face?*), she did just fine and adapted her remaining front leg to work in a piston-style hop. Again I was amazed by Duffy, her little man. When they were out together, he'd always walk on the side of the missing foot, as if to lend a hand in case she stumbled.

Later, when Bounty had healed, we'd watch the two dogs running in tandem over the many tailing piles or down the creek, chasing after something on a hunt. Just the two of them, side by side, soul mates brought together by the great matchmaker in the sky.

Their time together ran out in 1983, when Duffy died. Eight years later, due to Bounty's age and poor health, we had to put her down. She was sixteen years old and had shared a good, long life with us. We buried her deep in our garden behind the house at main camp. There isn't a time when we're planting or harvesting that part of the garden that I don't think of that big dog and the little terrier who was the love of her life. ✿

A Tale of Two Kitties
By Dexter Clark

Late one fall, just after Thanksgiving, we were driving some friends to the airport when they asked us to check on their cabin while they were Outside. As Robert Service wrote "...a pal's last need is a thing to heed," so we "swore we would not fail." They weren't sure how long they'd be gone, so they'd packed or stored their most important possessions.

First the holidays got in the way, then one thing or another, so it was late February before we got around to checking on their cabin, which was thirty miles east of Fairbanks. In the summer months, the two-mile trail into the cabin from the main road was usually four-wheel-drive only. Now that much-cursed trail laid beneath three feet of accumulated snow cover. We'd have to hoof it.

For the first mile or so, the going was easy, thanks to local snowmachiners leaving a well-packed pathway. This also was cause for concern about the cabin's security. Our worries eased somewhat at a fork in the trail; to the left was the trail to the cabin. There were no tracks in the fluffy white snow glistening in the sunlight. The intense brightness made us squint, so it seemed we were making faces at each other over the condition of the trail ahead. The easy-going was over.

We trudged through sometimes waist-deep snow for almost an hour before we rounded the last corner. Our fears of intruders were put to rest as their cabin came into view. It was still intact.

Truly an Alaskan homestead, the cabin was the epitome of living off the land. Store-bought lumber is expensive and a chore to haul into the site, so local trees were used as much as possible. Even though the largest log was only about three inches in diameter, the cabin was sturdy in its structure and utilitarian in design.

It was clear that no one had been near the cabin in quite a while, but we decided to check the inside, too, since we'd come so far. We used our feet to move back the snow that had accumulated around the door, and Yukon squeezed inside.

The interior of the cabin looked like a cyclone had hit it. The place had been ransacked. Then, a peculiar sound emanated from the supposedly empty cabin. A yeeoowl unlike we'd ever heard before!

"Sounds like there's a cat in here," Yukon said, and I squeezed in after her.

The noise was unmistakably the longest, loneliest and most pathetic meow ever made by a cat. The sound came from the loft area, and we looked up to see a medium-sized black cat emerge from beneath a wad of down-filled sleeping bags. It had found some refuge from the frigid air.

She looked as bad as she sounded when she trumpeted her "hello." She was very thin with ear tips missing and a tail a little shorter from the winter's freeze. Her fur looked like she had the worst case of kitty dandruff in history. And, man, was she glad to see someone, anyone!

Yukon picked the cat off the stairs and held it close, but the non-stop meowing continued.

We looked around the cabin trying to figure how she had survived so long. The cat climbed up on Yukon's shoulder and continued "talking" as if she were telling us the whole story of her winter. She would not quiet herself and would not leave Yukon's shoulder. She'd been left once before, and that certainly was not going to happen again.

As we went through the cabin, a picture of what may have happened started to form. All kinds of things were tipped off the shelves onto the floor. Every package that had ever held food was ripped open and any scraps consumed. We found a barrel of oats that looked like she had tried eating, then decided it was more fitting as a litter box.

Although our friends hadn't mentioned a missing cat, she must have been outside when they left. There was the cat door, completely blocked from the outside by falling snow. At some point she had returned only to be snowed in, literally.

We shut up the cabin — and the clean-up job our friends would face upon their return — and headed back along the trail with me in the lead and Yukon bringing up the rear. The trail we had created coming in made it easier going out, even with the cat perched on Yukon's shoulder, still telling the story that never ended, only now, to a much larger world.

When we got home, we put in a call to her traveling owners. After a week of phone tag, we learned that they would not be coming back in the foreseeable future. How would we like a cat? Her name is Amber.

Amber was, beyond a doubt, the toughest cat we ever had. Her exploits ranged from bringing home a weasel to feed her kittens, to putting down an adult Black Lab that had threatened them. Her former owners offered no explanation for her sudden change in attitude. With little debate, we kind of figured that Amber was just making sure she would never be forgotten, ever again.

Suffering Frostbite

Yukon's birthday was coming up, and she'd been pleading for another kitten. Amber and all of her kittens had passed on through various tragedies. So my sister Vickie and I went shopping. Pet Pride, a local kitty rescue club, had set up a display at the local mall, and there was only one kitty left. Okay, why not? Vickie coughed up half the twenty bucks.

The elderly lady who handled the sale was adamant about one thing: *If your wife doesn't like the cat, be sure and bring him back, no problem.* Even as we gathered up the yellow tabby, she repeated her money-back offer.

We still had Amber's litter box, so Vickie and I stopped and picked up some cat food and litter. When we got home, we left the kitty in the truck and went in to surprise Yukon. She saw the bag of food and shrieked, "Oh boy! I get to have a kitten!" Smiling, we suggested she go look in the front seat of the pick-up.

Yukon ran outside and was amazed to see the face of the hastily chosen present staring up at her from the base of the window.

"Where's his ears?" were her first words.

Vickie and I looked at each other with surprise and wonder. Then we both tried to peer into the truck's cab at the same time.

Where a kitty's ears usually are, there were little stumps of ears with just a few longer hairs growing out of them, giving the illusion of full-sized ears. The missing ears also lent to the illusion of having oversized eyes — two searchlights fixed on your face, unblinking and unnerving.

"So that's what that lady meant about you not liking the kitten. No problem. We can take it back."

By now Yukon had opened the truck door and gathered the nearly ear-less kitten into her arms. Then she noticed that his tail was a little shorter than normal.

"Frostbite" she said, "His name is Frostbite because that's what happened to his ears and tail."

It turns out that Frostbite, at almost six months old, was not exactly a kitten either. It was as if his early hardships had aged him. Even before he was two years old, we sometimes called him "The Old Man Cat."

That spring Frostbite became the main mining

Frostbite and I share the couch for an after-dinner catnap. His ailment stymied all the miners on the creek.

mouser. One morning, early into Frostbite's second year as a spoiled mining cat, Yukon felt him rubbing especially forcefully up against her as she lay in bed.

The crew was already in the pit, a lot of morning chores were done, and Yukon was just taking a little nap-type break. As she rubbed Frostbite's head, she realized that something was definitely out of the ordinary. A closer inspection revealed a serious problem with his jaw.

Yukon came down to the cut to talk to me about the cat's problem.

"I think his jaw's broken," she said.

"What can be done about it?"

"When a person breaks a jaw they have to eat everything through a straw for six months."

"I'm not feeding a cat through a straw for six months," I said. "If that's the case, he's one dead cat."

The veterinarian with the answer was more than a hundred miles away. Then we remembered that our new neighbors on the creek had a radio telephone. Perhaps they would let use it to call the vet.

The phone was located at the fanciest placer mining camp on any creek we'd ever worked or even seen. Originally the product of a gold mining investment scheme, their cook shack had been literally cut in half and moved about ten miles upstream to its present location. It featured a full commercial kitchen, hot showers, and flush toilets.

The current crew was new to the creek, but no strangers to the mining and construction business. They were leasing the camp and some nearby mining ground from our old partner, Sam.

We were unsure of our reception, and since we didn't see anyone around, we boldly knocked on the door of the camp's kitchen. We heard a muffled, "Come on in."

Inside, we introduced ourselves to an old "boomer." A boomer is the kind of guy who follows the boom side of a boom-and-bust economy. Traveling to wherever the work is, you'll find his counterpart at every construction site in the world. Today he was the only one left in camp.

He started out listening intently to our story.

"We've got a cat with a broken jaw. Could we use your radio-telephone to call town and find out if they can fix it? We'd be happy to pay for the call."

Some time passed. We had been expecting at least a grunt of yes or no. Maybe the boss told him not to let anyone use the phone. Had he even heard us?

He seemed to be distressed by something as he took off his welder's cap and scratched his head. One could sense a difficulty, but we didn't have a clue as to what he was thinking. It had to have been at least one full minute since we had made our request.

Suddenly, with what was probably divine inspiration, I said "It's a house cat."

Relief rushed in to the old man's face, replacing

the worried look. "Oh, hell yes, you can use the phone. I was just trying to figure out which part of the Cat you called the jaw."

Now we knew what the problem was. He had been searching his mind, going over every schematic he had ever seen, trying to figure out what these veteran miners were talking about, a jaw on a Cat. Was it a dozer or a loader?

On the phone, we found out that the vet could fix Frostbite, just bring him to town. We said our "thank yous" to our new friend, who was still laughing at himself for getting so wrapped up in the mechanical world.

When we got to the veterinarian's office in Fairbanks, we asked them what might have happened to cause the break. "Usually this is a sign that someone has kicked the cat."

We couldn't feature any of our crew doing this, so our best assumption was Frostbite had gotten in a spat with a moose or some other wild animal. Like the time we noticed the puncture wounds in his back apparently left by an unsuccessful attack by a hawk.

Frostbite had to stay overnight at the clinic, so we prepared to spend the rest of the day and night in town. First a phone call to a friend that acted as our liaison with town. Rich would take messages for us, store supplies in his refrigerator or freezer, and help with expediting whenever he was needed. His answering machine took the call. We left a message:

"We're in town. We've got a cat with a broken jaw. Looks like an overnighter. We'll call you later if we get the chance."

A trip to town is never a one-stop situation. We had several other items on the list. The first stop was at the equipment dealership, where we always bought parts for the General Motors machinery we used.

As we walked up to the parts counter, the smiling clerk asked us in his familiar manner. "What brings you guys to town?"

"Broken jaw on the cat."

For the second time that day, we saw a bewildered look on a face in response to our statement. This time we knew what was going on, so we let the young man struggle with schematics for a while before saying, "It's a house cat."

Once again, the same relief replaced the frown on the brow.

"I was just going to get the parts book out and have you show me what you needed."

As it went there, so went the entire trip. In every encounter that we mentioned a "cat with a broken jaw," it was assumed we were talking about a piece of machinery.

Even our friend who heard it on his answering machine message got the wrong idea. He told us later that he woke up out of a sound sleep that night with the thought, "But they don't run Caterpillar. They've got Terex."

Frostbite's jaw was wired up, and he looked fine the next morning, unaware of the fun we were having at his expense. His food had to be softened, but he could eat on his own. We were told to bring him back in six weeks for removal of the pin.

Frostbite was unaffected by the entire event other than being restricted to camp. Our mama dog Bounty had a fresh litter of puppies, which got most of the attention anyway. We checked with the crew for possible causes of the break. Did the door slam on the cat? Did anyone kick at the cat? Does anyone know what might have happened? No, no, and no!

We didn't find out what likely happened until the day we got back from town after the wire was removed. Frostbite, still groggy from the veterinarian's drugs, came too close to Bounty's latest litter. Yukon watched in horror as the dog growled a warning, then snapped at the cat, catching his head in her mouth. It was hardly a bite, but it was enough.

In a moment, the surgeon's skill, and month and a half of healing, was undone. The cat's jaw hung limply like before.

This time when we went to the vet, at least we had some answers. Although we accepted full responsibility, they were sympathetic. Even though they had to repeat the operation, they only charged us half price.

Back at the mine, we fell into our same routine, but now we were extra careful to keep Frostbite away from Bounty and her puppies.

Mining season was over before it was time for our unfortunate feline to have the pin removed from his jaw. The vet was confident that we had a healing. Less than a week later, Frostbite presented himself to Yukon, for the third time, with his chin on his chest.

This time the vet decided to put in a very small king pin that wouldn't require removal. Best of all, this time there was no charge.

Frostbite carried that pin to his grave nearly ten years later. He had been a good cat so we laid him to rest in our garden. It seemed right that the old orange tabby be placed beneath the carrot bed. To this day whenever we show friends or visitors our productive carrot patch, we end up telling the story of the cat with a broken jaw. ✿

A Fitting Farewell
By Yukon Yonda

The knock at the door so early was odd. We'd come home late the night before and had talked of sleeping in late. But a knock at that hour usually meant someone needed help. Dexter flashed out of bed and down the stairs to answer the door. Seconds later, he called back upstairs to me, saying it was our neighbors from 10 Mile, Cal and Ray.

I wanted to snuggle back down in the covers knowing I would have the time to nap while they visited over the first pot of coffee. Finally, deciding to put the time to better use, I threw back the covers. Looking out the front windows onto a beautiful winter morning, I thought it odd I'd not yet smelled brewing coffee, and the house seemed strangely hushed.

There was a quiet conversation ongoing at the front door, then Bountiful, upstairs with me, threw back her head and gave out the most mournful, woeful howl. My eyes flashed around the room. *Duffy! Where was Duffy?* I raced into some clothes and leaped for the stairs. As soon as I hit the landing and saw Dexter's face my heart stopped. Dexter then wrapped his arms around me to share this worst of news. Duffy was dead.

I can't begin to relate the feelings that rushed over me. Anyone who has shared that experience just knows. After the initial shock came a few answers. Cal and Ray, both mushers from Howling Spirit Kennel, had found Duffy when they were out feeding their team in their dog yard. In working kennels, the dog houses are separated by circles of territory, defined by the length of each dog's chain. They'd found Duffy just inside the circle of Doofus, one of their leaders. Duffy was dead, frozen through with a hellacious snarl on his face. It appeared his neck was broke clean. Simply put, Duffy was in the wrong place at the wrong time, and had been killed during a territorial challenge.

My mind was racing: *What had Duffy been doing in the dog yard, and how did he get there?* We lived three miles away, so it wasn't far to travel, and he was used to being at their cabin. Dexter and I had helped as sled dog handlers for their kennel, so we were there often. But he wasn't known to travel much without one of his people. Then it hit. I'd been bartending that night at the Cliff House, a Fox saloon not far from the kennel. When Dexter came to pick me up, he'd brought Duffy along. We had stayed over a while to visit on the other side of the bar with Duffy under the my stool. At some point Duffy must have slipped outside and headed to the familiar territory his humans frequented.

Cal and Ray were heartsick. They'd been friends of ours for years, and this was news they had not wanted to carry. Even before they came this morning, they'd built a pine box for Duffy. Knowing the ground would be impossible for grave-digging until the end of May (if we were lucky), we decided to clear space for the pine box out back in our utility freezer. That would keep him until spring, then he'd go out to camp for burial. That's where he belonged.

By the time winter came to an end, and the season rolled around, we had grand plans for this mining dog and the burial honors he had coming.

The first month of that mining season was different from previous years. Winter had brought an odd spring. Thawing and re-freezing had glaciered the Harrison, valley wall to valley wall. Usually the creek road was accessible and mining could be in full swing by the end of May. This year we figured if the ice was gone by the Fourth of July, we'd be lucky. We had to doze our way around just to get settled into camp. And here we were with one very dead dog needing services.

The year before, working a side cut in the valley, Dexter had come across the remains of an old wooden flume system that old-timers had used to move water to the sluice box in a low-water season. Always ready to recycle, Dexter spent the extra time to pile what remained of the flume off to the side of the creek, stacking it where we'd already mined. This woodpile figured highly in the burial rites we'd been planning for Duffy, and there it was, encased in spring glacier. Our plan was to use it as a funeral pyre and give Duffy a heck of a send-off, complete with pyrotechnics. We'd always remember this dog as a gunpowder-eating fireworks fool, who couldn't stay away from lift-offs, even if it meant singeing his muzzle. In the weeks following every Fourth of July, Duffy sported an uneven beard.

As always in the Arctic, having a Plan B is of utmost importance. Since we couldn't bury or cremate Duffy just yet, we organized the "dead-dog detail" in camp. Twice a day, somebody had to cover Duffy's little pine box with enough glacier ice to keep his remains refrigerated until that ancient woodpile thawed out.

Wendall, one of our long-time hands and Duffy's oldest friend (besides me), volunteered immediately. Morning and night, faithfully, Wendall took up his task after his camp responsibilities were completed. He would trek out to the glacier across the creek and dump more ice on Duffy's coffin.

As luck would have it, the weather turned, and the woodpile began to dry in the full spring sun. Two weeks later, the ice gave up its trophy, and we were able to continue with our plans. In that time we'd made a trip into town for the few things that had missed the list coming out to camp.

On the way back from town, we made a short stop at 101 Mile to pick out some of Duffy's favorite fireworks: bottle rockets, Roman candles, buzz bombs, busy bees, and more. The next day, with everything assembled for Duffy's send-off, the crew gathered by the funeral site. Dexter placed Duffy's box in the center of the old woodpile, and we liberally sprinkled the fire-crackers on the wood, along with about ten gallons of dirty diesel fuel to help things along.

Four of us — me, Dexter, Ray, and Wendall — circled the woodpile with Roman candles in hand. On Dexter's signal, we lit our torches and pointed them at the pile. The spark from my candle ignited the wood. Each of us was lost in thought and memories of the good times with this little furry friend — how his antics and companionship had earned him the title of full mining partner in our camp. It was a blaze seldom seen, and the explosions and whistling fireworks created a thrilling blast of sound, like the end of an Independence Day show when they let everything go at once.

Long after the last of the fireworks exploded, the fire crackled and burned. Then, after about ten minutes, a single red ball arched out of the flames, a lone rocket that somehow wasn't ignited during the big burst. To me, it seemed like a sign from my old friend, and I felt some comfort.

"He's still heading north," I thought, "and if ever we cross paths again, I know I'll recognize a good mining dog when I see one."

Two days later, the ashes had cooled enough so that our ceremony could be completed. I gathered some of "him" and placed the ashes on a little firecracker boat for a trip down the sluice box, and ultimately out to the Yukon River. Of canine, not Viking breed, Duffy had earned a voyage to Valhalla nonetheless. ✿

TRICIA BROWN

In 1984, Yukon and I embarked in a new direction as lodge operators and as foster parents.

8

Change of Life

By Dexter Clark

We did not set any wheels in motion to have a foster daughter. She took the initiative. It was Easter 1984. Tammi had been placed in the state's custody after some serious problems in her family, and she was living in a church group home in Fairbanks.

Easter Sunday was cause for special celebration, and several of the kids from the home were riding in a van out past our place. Tammi asked, or rather told, the van driver, "Pull in that driveway! I know these people."

In the house, we were just sitting down to our Easter dinner. "Who's this, pulling in with a van?" We all turned our attention out the windows to see a small girl, ill-dressed for the cold, scampering up to our front door. Yukon let the little girl into the house, where it was warmer. It turned out we knew her and her family, but we knew nothing of their recent travails.

With those in the van waiting patiently, she burst forth with a flood of words, like people in dangerous situations tend to talk after the danger has passed. The best information we could get was her address at the church home, and a schedule for visiting hours. She begged us to come visit. *And by the way could you adopt me, or be my foster parents, or something?*

She might have been there all of ten minutes, then like a flower at the first frost, she was gone.

We sat down to eat as if little orphans came to our door every day and asked for us to adopt them. We made plans to go see what we could to do help her.

The group home was a shock to us from our first visit. Fourteen juvenile adolescent boys on one side and the same number of hormone-driven girls on the other, with a common area for cooking, eating, recreation (one TV), discipline area (time-out room), and staff offices.

We all sat at a table to talk at a slower speed, with time for questions. A sign on the wall listed the rules. Rule number three in particular caught our eye for it said: "No Fornication." Not a nice atmosphere for a young lady trying to grow up.

We decided to bust her out of there no matter what. But it took weeks just to get permission for her to stay overnight. Hardest of all was the three months of filling out forms. We wanted to be honest, yet we knew to give them some of the answers they wanted to hear.

One of the questions was "What are your goals?" Since these were separate applications, we each had trouble with individual goals in a marriage situation. My answer was the shortest: "When I grow up, I want to be ninety-five years old."

Yukon and I had hoped to get Tammi out before we left for Harrison Creek that mining season. We were told about the "home study" that must take place within two weeks of the child being placed in a home. But by the time they were ready for the home study phase, we were already at the mine.

The day the social services inspector was due at Harrison Creek, it had been raining for several days. As a result, the creeks were raging full of water, and we had our doubts about her coming. The mining road crosses the creek several times, and to a greenhorn, the road seems to just disappear. I decided to take the truck out to the Steese to meet her.

She was a little late, but pretty plucky. I left her Reliant K car at the Miller House, a lodge up on the highway, and opted to take her in the four-wheel-drive. She admitted she would have never attempted it alone.

By the time we got into the mine, it was a sunshine day. We went over the regulations one by one. Separate room

Each spring, glaciers and high water made our first trips out to the mine a dangerous endeavor.

for the child's privacy. We'd given her the loft over the pantry where we used to sleep. A curtain hung down from the ceiling all around. A combination rope ladder with two-by-fours for steps led up to her little loft. In case of fire, we'd hung a big, knotted rope out the small window. Tammi willingly demonstrated how it worked.

Next the woman needed a water sample, so Yukon and I took our guest down to the clear water of Maiden Pup, our only water source. She was amazed when we just scooped her sample jar into the untreated creek water and handed it to her.

The most awkward moment came as we were watching her fill out her papers. Yukon was pouring her a cup of coffee when the woman's eyes caught sight of the gun rack that held two rifles and a shotgun.

"Are those guns loaded?" she asked pointedly.

Our old aluminum camp coffee pot had fallen victim to a curious black bear during the previous winter. The bear's bite was clearly visible in the bottom and side of the pot. Since the bear hadn't bitten all the way through, the coffee pot was still serviceable. As soon as we pointed out the teeth marks, our somewhat sobered visitor turned back to filling out the papers.

Despite our outward calm during the inspection,

we nervously awaited the mail plane until we got an "Official Use Only" envelope from the state with the results inside. The water was fine, privacy was acceptable, and "Bear bites in the coffee pot make a convincing argument for a waiver to have loaded guns on site."

We passed. We had us a daughter.

Mining camp is as good as a farm for raising children. Our partner's son, Shawn, was a couple years younger than Tammi. This gave each of them another kid to hang around with, and both were willing helpers.

Unfortunately, Tammi got caught in the crossfire when another decision we'd made in early 1984 caught up with us. We were mining without the protection of a discharge permit. Various industries, such as ours, must apply for permits that allow certain levels of pollutants to enter the waters of the United States. Our position was that earth itself is not a pollutant, so we didn't need the permit. Since we never tried to keep this a secret, it was a matter of when, not if, we would face consequences. The Environmental Protection Agency determined that our mining days were over — for now.

After the shutdown, we regrouped and made plans for a future with our foster daughter. There was never a question of letting her go "back to the state." But Yukon and I had qualms about her newly emerging personality being confronted with a large high school system like the one in Fairbanks. That wasn't going to cut it.

We'd heard about an opportunity to run the Central Lodge, a spacious log restaurant and bar combination with rental cabins. The lodge was once the center of social life in Central. When telephone service finally arrived, the lodge got one first. Gasoline, diesel fuel, propane, and fresh water were other good reasons for locals and travelers alike to stop at the lodge.

When we first found out the lodge was up for sale, we didn't give it a second thought. But now things were different. Without a liveli-hood, cooking and bartending was more appealing. Yukon and I arranged to man-age and lease the lodge in Central for one year. We moved from the mine directly into one

Yukon helping Tammi with her homework. I called my girls "The Gaggettes."

of several cabins on the property. Since the entire place was heated with wood, we arranged for some locals to trade firewood for food and beverages. School was about two hundred yards away, and Tammi's enrollment brought the total to an even dozen students that year.

As usual when starting in a new location we cleaned and cleaned. Yukon and I scraped a bushel of "Johnson's One Step" wax off the hardwood floor. I set about rebuilding the generator for more reliable power in the coming winter. And we joined the local church, with services at Circle Hot Springs, eight miles away.

Right away it became apparent that when the miners left Central in the fall, they took most of the economy with them. It was going to be a tight winter, but we had to hold on until spring. When the miners returned, business would be better

Yukon, Tammi, and I all settled in to the work-ings of the lodge. Tammi helped us with the cleaning and cooking. We adults took turns behind the bar, even getting one of our mining partners to help.

Then, another challenge: While I was waiting for parts I'd ordered to rebuild the generator, the back-up generator quit working. We resorted to using the welder from the mine. By only running it during business hours, we saved on diesel. It was the talk of the town how we kept the place open with that welder for a generator.

Things were getting real tight by mid-January. The last thing we needed was one more problem. That's when the sewer froze up. It would cost about a thousand dollars to get a pumping and thawing company from Fairbanks to drive out to Central in the middle of winter. There was no way. But without a septic tank, how could we keep the place open for business?

Our solution was to intercept the main sewage line in the basement of the lodge. We redirected the sewage into a fifty-five gallon drum. A screened overflow, near the top of the drum, allowed excess liquids to flow off into a five-gallon bucket with a sump pump inside. The liquids were pumped out and well away from the lodge to the spot chosen for next year's garden.

We fondly referred to our ingenious solution as "a floating crap game going on down in the basement." Come spring we borrowed a small track loader, dug up the faulty septic, and replaced it with an old fuel tanker.

That same spring, the building where the local Baptist congregation met was needed for another purpose, but only for a month. Where would we have church? There weren't that many places that could hold the congregation of about twenty-five, so we volunteered the use of the lodge for Sunday morning services. Many were skeptical, but they had little choice.

The first time we gathered in the saloon, the preacher brought his chalkboard, and we propped it up on the pool table against a few cases of beer. As soon as he called for a blessing, however, the atmosphere changed dramatically. As rough and rugged as the lodge was, this was our place of worship. After church, everyone agreed that the lodge was a good place as any. We made only one request of the congregation: Please don't

Central artist Carol Gelvin painted this reclining "nude" for the bar. I only asked that Carol put a dress on her.

circle the saloon seven times while singing.

The gold miners returned with the spring thaw, and business began to pick up once more. We had decided early on that we would serve a limited menu: dinners on the weekends and a maybe sandwiches to fill in the gaps. The question was what to serve. What would attract the locals over the winter and draw the miners into town during their season? Fish fry on Friday was an easy choice with beer batter on halibut chunks. A friend suggested prime rib for Saturday night. "Then you serve barbecued ribs on Sunday," he said. Since we'd never made a prime rib, he gave us some pointers.

That first roast got more attention than a woman birthing a baby. We were nervous not only about the quality, but that seven-rib roast cost nearly $50. *Well*, we thought, *if we don't sell it we can always have barbecued beef sandwiches*. The fifteen dinners from that wonderful chunk of beef sold out in less than a half-hour. A new Saturday night ritual had arrived in Central.

As shy as she was, Tammi wouldn't even try waitressing. But after she saw the kind of tips another local girl was getting, she bravely faced her fear, eventually becoming our best helper. She seldom complained about the mountain of dishes that had to be washed when the dining tapered off.

Our reputation for excellent food and good service grew each weekend. We perfected the prime rib technique until we were fixing four roasts every Saturday night. The secret was in the au jus that we started a day earlier. The parts of the vegetables you might normally throw away went into the pot — onions and the skins, carrots with their tops, the base of bunch of celery, cauliflower cores, stems and pieces of mushrooms, and broccoli bits. We let this simmer until all the vegetables turned to mush, then it was strained. Soy sauce and garlic juice were added when we were starting to prep the meat itself. After searing the roast to soften the fat, we used a hypodermic needle to inject about a cup of the au jus into the meat. Yum yum.

There was sadness on many fronts when the miners left that fall. Although the business had been successful, the owner returned to take over. We had little choice but to return to our home and headquarters in Fox, wondering "What next?"

As we suspected, the high school in the big city of Fairbanks was more than Tammi could handle. Within a month of her enrollment she had fallen in with the wrong crowd. We overreacted with parental admonishments about the difference between friends and acquaintances. Then one day at school she contacted the state officials in charge of foster care and asked to be placed in a different home. As heart-breaking as it was for Yukon and me, we accepted her decision with the knowledge of having done our best to help her.

We didn't hear from Tammi for more than a year, but of course we wondered about her often. Then one day she called. She had quit school and was going through some rough times. It was clear that she wanted to talk out her troubles with adults she could trust.

Our daughter Tammi and grandbaby Racquel. We're a complete family.

After that, Tammi called us regularly. We were so proud when she told us she'd earned her GED diploma. Then came her first job, working in a restaurant. And later, when Tammi married, she included us in the wedding.

Today Tammi has a daughter of her own, and she's teaching her little one to call us Grandma and Grandpa. A friend of ours who knew we'd never had any children of our own asked us, "How'd you get to be grandparents without ever being parents?"

"The same way you avoid diapers, measles, mumps, teething, and potty training," I told him. "Get 'em when they're thirteen."

We still laugh about those days when we were gold miners-turned-innkeepers. But our memories hold more than a bunch of stories. We learned valuable lessons about family, and about community, in Central. As for our prime rib dinners, the people we served there still ask when we're going to open another restaurant. The answer? *Not while there's gold to be dug.* ✿

TRICIA BROWN

Our long-time mining partner, Bob Jones, checks the test riffle for pay dirt. Even in late spring, Jones is in his bunny boots.

Two Burly Miners Get Their Wings

By Dexter Clark

It was a typical, early winter, late afternoon in the Interior of Alaska; cold and getting dark. We were anxiously awaiting the arrival of our dear friend and mining partner, Bob Jones. Four hours earlier, he'd phoned ahead from the village of Central to let us know he was on his way into town. He should have been here by now. If he didn't show up or call us in the next hour, we would go looking for him.

We were especially concerned because of the reason for his coming. Briefly, on the phone, he had told us his mother was gravely ill, and he needed to go to Denver to be at her side. We prayed for both of them as we waited.

Bob fits most city dwellers' image of an Alaskan the way that John Wayne typifies the all-American cowboy. Bob started out as a squatter in a self-made dugout with a half-cabin, then he homesteaded forty acres in a state land disposal in the Crazy Mountains near Central. Mining for gold in the summer, running a trapline on snowmachine in the winter, building his own log cabin, meeting all the state's requirements for "proving up" on the homestead, and raising a family in the Bush. It all contributed to his look. His physical characteristics reinforce this impression because Bob is just plain a big guy, almost six feet tall, weighing in well over two hundred pounds during the good years. Being hairy helps, sporting full facial fur and a two-foot ponytail, he would appear to be out of place just about anywhere else in the United States.

When Bob pulled into our driveway about half an hour later, we were so relieved that we ran outside, despite the cold, to greet him. His story unfolded even before he got out of the truck. Eagle Summit was in white-out conditions, (white-out occurs when blowing snow blends with the snow on the ground until it is difficult to see more than a few feet in front of your vehicle), so he had wisely followed the state maintenance vehicle over the pass. Hence his tardiness.

Bob grabbed his grip out of his pickup and we hurried toward the house. Unlike us, he was dressed for the cold, wearing his bunny boots. Anyone who has ever had cold feet in their life would love this military surplus Arctic footwear. With a white rubber outer shell, they make your feet look three sizes bigger, but they're oh-so-warm. Once Bob put those boots on in the fall, they were the only shoes, if you could call them that, on his feet until after breakup.

The rest of Bob was well-layered, starting with long johns — which suffered the same ever-present fate as his bunny boots — a flannel shirt, a heavy wool shirt or a light jacket, and topped off with his down parka, complete with several duct tape patches. He had been stranded out in the Arctic cold before and was taking no chances. Only Bob's billed cap with some mining logo was not survival-type gear, but we knew there was a ski mask in one of those parka pockets. So, to say Bob is the stereotypical, rough hewn, model Alaskan gold miner is to infer that water just might be wet.

We said quick hellos and rushed into the warm comfort of our home, The Biosphere, where we spend our winters. We're on seven acres of patented mining ground two miles from downtown Fox, a town that the federal government calls a "census designated place."

That is to say there is no official government, no fire protection, and certainly no shopping centers or malls in Fox. So our source for most supplies and services is still Fairbanks.

As we sipped hot coffee to ward off the chill, Bob grabbed the phone to make some arrangements. First he called the travel agent to book the flight, then he reached his state-side family to let them know his itinerary. Once we knew his schedule, we got ready for a trip into town to pick up his ticket.

Our trip started like any other this time of year: Start the car and let it warm up for at least fifteen minutes. The '51 Chevy was our daily driver, summer and winter. For safe starts in cold weather, our cars are all equipped with block heaters and oil pan heaters with a standard 110-volt plug hanging out of the grille. Several hours of preheating are required in temperatures down to twenty below and, after that, the vehicle is often plugged in the night before a trip to town. In minus-forty or colder, the car may be plugged in for days at a time. To combat the cold in the old Chevy's interior we'd installed an auxiliary heater that keeps it comfortable, but you might not want to take off your coat.

We both bundled up this time. We were in a hurry to get into the travel agent before their office closed, so when Yukon handed us a list on the way out the door, I pocketed it without noticing the cardboard box label that was attached.

We trusted the Chevy, but I made sure we had a pair of insulated coveralls in the back seat in case of problems. In Interior Alaska, you don't travel far without essential survival gear. Most people have a bag or box in the trunk of their car containing extra gear to protect against the cold in case of emergency.

Ah, winter in Alaska: Four-thirty in the afternoon and it was totally dark outside.

"It's twenty-five below." Bob's simple sentence summed up the weather as he lumbered into the car. The thermometer hanging on our open air front porch attracts more attention as the mercury dips lower and lower. Since the temperature is the only part of the weather that changes much in winter, we check it as religiously as a Moslem called to prayer.

The car was warm inside as we pulled out onto the Steese Highway. The tires still had little flat spots in them, just on the bottoms, of course, from sitting in the cold. So, characteristic of the first few miles of any trip in the winter, we were bump, bump, bumping our way toward town. As the tires started to round out, we increased our speed. The air in the car cooled as the frigid outside air found its way through weather stripping that was forty-plus years old.

On the way into town, we speculated about his mother's condition and never gave the shopping list a second thought. Bob's mom had been placed on life-support, and the family was talking about keeping that going until Bob could get there. It had been several years since he'd been Outside to see his relatives, and he already had a ticket for a trip in the early spring. This unexpected jaunt was going to crimp his budget.

As our breath added humidity to the Chevy's interior, frost began to build on the windows, slowly squeezing our environment until just two half-moons of clear visibility remained in the windshield. The atmosphere in that car contributed to a closeness that surpassed fifteen years of friendship and working together.

I related an old cliché to try to ease Bob's mind: "Worrying is like rocking in a rocking chair. It gives you something to do, but it doesn't get you anywhere." He just responded with a grunting sound like a cross between an old bull moose and a harbor seal. Well, he'd probably heard all my little cheer-up proverbs over the years, so we drove the rest of the way to town in silence, each of us lost in our thoughts.

We made it to the travel agent's office with five minutes to spare, and Bob rushed in to get his ticket. I waited in the car to make sure it kept running. We were parked right out front and the women in the office were obviously admiring the old Chevy. They were pointing the car out to others in the office and asking Bob about it. There is no doubt, if you want to get attention, just drive an old car, especially in Fairbanks in the winter.

Back in the car, Bob again checked the departure time of his flight. We had about three hours, plenty of time to do the shopping before heading for the airport. We'd get done quicker with his help. So we went about Fairbanks in our usual circuit, saving groceries for last so that any perishables would spend the least time in the car and face less risk of freezing. A couple of quick stops later, and we were heading for the market.

As we pulled into the grocery store parking lot, we decided to both go in, which meant leaving the car locked and running with the throttle pulled out a little. The only real threat was overheating caused by a piece of cardboard in front of the radiator, standard equipment for most older vehicles during Alaska's harsh winters. Everything is fine as long as you're cruising down the highway, but sitting and idling required removing the cardboard for a short time. With that accomplished, we headed inside.

The bright fluorescent store lights were a stunning contrast to the dark world outside. Looking more like bewildered refugees than a couple of burly miners we grabbed a shopping cart and started down the first aisle with Bob in charge of the list. A quick read-through in his usual, deep, gruff voice ended abruptly as he said "panty liners." Immediately, he detached the mysterious cardboard box label to reveal the product manufacturer, trade name and, most importantly, the prominent feature: wings. An unquestioned, unspoken decision was reached to leave that item for last.

All too quickly, every other thing on the list was in the cart, and we headed for No Man's Land, the aisle known as feminine hygiene.

As soon as we were out of sight of the other shoppers, Bob handed me the label to compare to the products on the shelf. I shoved it in my pocket as I had already seen enough of that label to know IT should be easy to spot on the shelf. A once-over glance at the shelf stirred a sinking feeling in my stomach. They did not have the right kind. I had no choice but to pull the crumpled label out of my pocket, straighten it and begin comparing, brand by brand, with the products on the shelf. There were maxis and minis, lite days and ultra-lights (until now I thought that was a new kind of an airplane). Finally I saw the key word "wings." The manufacturer was different, but I figured we'd been in this aisle long enough. I tossed the box in the cart.

Bob was trying to be helpful in his own way and noticed another brand of "wings," which he took off the shelf. He took the box out of the cart to compare them, feature by feature.

Just then, the nose of another cart came around the corner. Until then, we had been alone in the aisle. The cart was piloted by a boy of about twelve, followed by his father. We only had to move our cart a little to let them by, but Bob had his hands full, so I ended up dragging the cart sideways and letting them pass. They cruised past, pretending not to notice what we were doing. Just as they left the aisle, I heard the boy ask, "What are they buying those for, Dad?"

I just wanted out of the store. If Bob had left my first choice in the cart, we'd be gone by now. I told Bob to put "his choice" back on the shelf and "my choice" back in the cart, which he did, then walked ahead. It was obvious that he was through pushing the cart, so we headed for the checkout with me at the helm. The box of panty-liners was out of sight, beneath a loaf of bread.

I planned the checkout carefully and made sure the object of our embarrassment would be the last item to ring up. The middle-aged clerk was chosen for not knowing us and was a paragon of efficiency, bagging the groceries as she scanned them. This was perfect.

Finally she reached into the cart and picked up the loaf of bread. "Was that a gasp?" I wondered. No, just me finally breathing. It was almost over.

"I think these are on sale, sir," she said with what seemed to be a leer. This could well have been the only time in the world I did not want to hear those words. Bob was busy studying supermarket tabloids and *Cosmopolitan* magazine.

"Just a second, I'll check," the woman said as she reached for the intercom phone. I wanted to interrupt: "Please, don't do that. I'll pay full price." But a lifetime of bragging about bargains caused me to hesitate. The dreaded words went into the microphone, broadcasting to everyone in the store: "Register seven, price check on StayFree panty-liners with wings."

I wondered if the father and son were still in the store. Maybe back by the dairy section rolling in the aisle. I noticed that Bob had taken a sudden interest in the different kinds of dog food stockpiled in the front of the store, even though the brand he fed his dog was not sold here. It seemed an eternity before a teen-aged girl with a too-wide a smile showed up to grab the box of panty liners and run back to check the price. She could have said they were ten dollars for all I know. I quickly paid the bill and led the way out of the store.

Back in the car, we argued a bit about whose fault it was that we had such a humbling experience.

Bob recalled a similar incident back when he was still married, and by the time we arrived at the airport, we were both able to see some humor in the whole thing. After I saw Bob off, I paid the parking fee and headed out for home.

As the cold crept back into the car, thoughts crowded my mind. At first I was concerned about Bob's flight safety, then the welfare of his mother and the rest of his family. I pictured Bob telling them about how things were going in Alaska. But I just couldn't feature him telling them about our adventure at the market.

As I previewed the story I had for Yukon about our suffering over those doggone "wings," I laughed right out loud. I knew she'd think it hilarious. I realized, too, that Bob would have a tale to cheer his family.

As the old Chevy carried me closer and closer to home, I thought about how Bob was more than a little inconvenienced by the sudden need to go Outside. Then it occurred to me: Was there such a big difference between what we had done for Yukon and what he was doing for his mother and others in his family?

My reasoning had rolled around until it snagged on the motive for each of our actions tonight. Right now, although separated by hundreds of miles, traveling in opposite directions, Bob and I were both going to the same place — home — to those we love and who love us. ✿

Found and Lost
By Dexter Clark

It's been said before, "Of all the things I've lost, it's my mind I miss the most." For a fellow who's lost lots of gold from time to time, this is a hard statement to make, yet I stand by it.

The first big loss was definitely intended to be a lesson learned. We had a pretty nice clean-up, so it was time for a town trip, although even poor or so-so clean ups lead to town trips. The cut we were working had not been producing very many good-sized nuggets, but this time there were enough that we put the largest ones in a gold pan and took a Polaroid snapshot.

One nugget, larger than the rest, caught my eye and imagination. I was pretty sure that beautiful nugget weighed just over half an ounce, though in discussions since then, it has gained weight, often described as "an ounce." Or if Yukon is around, it was "over an ounce."

The nugget attracted so much attention because of its peculiar shape — very flat with the thickness of an old silver dollar. That in itself wasn't so odd, but near one end there was a hole all the way through it. That made for discussion of putting a precious stone, maybe a ruby or garnet, in the hole, like it was made to be.

After the picture was taken, the nugget slipped into my pocket and felt like it belonged there. *Mine!* Not my biggest, but my new favorite.

That nugget stayed in that pocket all the way into town only because I didn't make any stops, so there was no one to show it to for their appreciation or evaluation. As I recall, Yukon had stayed in camp, so any problems on this trip would be my responsibility alone.

My first stop was an auto parts store where I did a lot of business, so I was recognized as soon as I entered the place. I couldn't wait to show off my latest find. As soon as one of the counter guys came over to help me, I reached in my pocket, drew out my new precious treasure and plopped it down on the parts counter.

"You think maybe I could gets some parts with this?" I wisecracked.

The clerk's eyes were agog as he picked up the nugget to admire it. He tossed it from hand to hand as others in the store crowded around to look. In the old days, this was probably not such an uncommon sight, but for most of the workers here, it was there first look at a genuine, newly found, gold nugget.

I will admit to a certain amount of pride at my nugget being the center of attention, so with a little reluctance, I put it back in my pocket and went about my business according to my list.

At each stop after that, the same scenario was repeated. Bring out the nugget, brag a little about putting a stone in it, then slip it back in my pocket and slide on out of there.

As lunch was approaching, I met some friends in one of the stores and we decided to go to our favorite pizza place. This time I held off showing the nugget until we were all seated, the pizza was ordered, and we were faced with filling the time waiting for the order to be filled. Pulling out the nugget and flipping it out on the table, like the dollar it resembled, felt pretty good. There was no sense of impending doom at all.

My friends were still "oohing and aahing" when the pizza arrived, and we realized some things in life are more important than some gold nugget. Like hunger.

I slipped the nugget back into my pocket past the tail of my shirt which was hanging outside of my pants because it was a very warm day in Fairbanks.

We finished the meal, which I paid for, left a nice tip and went our separate ways. My first stop was the bank,

The distinctive look of each nugget we find makes it forever special. Sometimes we name them for their shapes.

the last place in the world to haul out any gold, so I never bothered with it there. With the banking done, I headed for the general merchandise store to see how much more of the list I could scratch off.

I had just started shopping when I ran into the new wife of a dear friend I'd worked with on the Trans-Alaska Pipeline. After the preliminary, how're you doing, how's married life, I decided to show her my latest find. I stuffed my hand down into my right pants pocket and came out with a different, smaller nugget that I had almost forgotten I had in there. Then I felt a bit of panic. Where's the BIG one?

Down to the bottom of the pocket went my hand, fishing around, but to no avail. That pocket was empty, and there was no hole in it either. *Maybe I put it in another pocket.* So I looked in each and every pocket, all with the same result, no nuggets in there. By now, that really sinking feeling you get when something has gone awry had entered my entire body.

"It's gone. I think I've lost it," I gasped. "I've got to go look for it."

My friend's wife tried to be helpful, "Where were you when you last had it?"

I was a little rude, for I left my cart with the few things in it, and my friend's wife, right then and there. I headed for the pizza place first because that was the last place I remembered having it out of my pocket.

I ran into the restaurant and cornered our wait-ress, "Has any one turned in a gold nugget? Did you or anyone here find a gold nugget?" I realized how foolish I sounded as the words tumbled out. She tried to be helpful, but shook her head. No, no, sure hadn't.

We pulled out all the chairs from around the table where we had eaten. I crawled around on the floor going over every inch of the carpet as if I were looking for a contact lens.

Less than an hour ago, I'd held that nugget at this very spot. I felt my chances of finding it slipping away. Gloom and dread remained. No luck. Or should I say lots of luck, all of it bad.

Once the interior was diligently searched, I looked around the parking lot where the truck had been parked. During this process, I started to figure out what may have happened. The tail of my T-shirt was still flapping in the breeze as I went to dig the truck keys out of my pocket. My hand caught in the tail, which then accompanied my hand into the pocket. I readily retrieved the keys, but the tail of the shirt stayed in the pocket, until I actually got in the truck.

I'll bet that's what happened, I thought. I'd tucked my shirt tail into the pocket along with that nugget. When that tail worked its way out of there, it brought the nugget out with it. So I searched the cab of the truck, in, around and under the seat. Not there!

Next I drove to the bank and repeated my parking lot search to no avail. By now I had done enough ground-searching and soul-searching to come to a few conclusions. First of all, God had gotten me for bragging about our wonderful find. I didn't make that nugget. He had. I'd merely found it.

By now, someone else had most likely found it again, so my chances of recovery were very minuscule. That someone, I decided, was probably a tourist from Iowa, who was calling his family back home at this very minute (*You won't believe what I found today!*), encouraging them to move to Alaska because gold nuggets were just lying around on the streets.

Every time I see a similar piece of gold hanging around someone's neck, I move in for a closer look. No, I won't ask for the nugget back, even though I still have that snapshot to show that I was the first finder. I just want to hear their side of the story.

If it's "finder's keepers, loser's weepers," why ain't I cryin'? Instead of focusing on my loss, I imagine the joy in the heart and life of the finder. I know that joy by my own experience.

The gold will outlast us all. It will be around long after the stories are forgotten and the photographs have faded. Somehow that idea is comforting. ✿

*Bob Jones and I pull up the test riffles at The Biosphere mine site.
Beyond us are two souvenirs from the old days that we've relocated to
our patented ground outside Fairbanks: our cook shack from Harrison
Creek, and the sign from "Yukon Yonda's Central Roadhouse."*

The Biosphere
By Dexter Clark

For a person driving by on the Steese Highway, our place looks like a transplanted Western movie saloon or an old general store. We're used to people pulling in to ask "Is this someplace?" or "Didn't this used to be something?" or even "Are you open today?" Some ask for directions, chat for a minute, or take a few pictures before they leave. Then there's the muddled locals, some of whom insist this place has been around for fifty years or more. Actually, it's only thirty years old, but it stood empty, forlorn and unfinished, for most of its early life — until we claimed it.

TRICIA BROWN

Each of us fell in love with the unusual house even before we met. Together, we conceived a plan to make it our home.

Long before Yukon and I met, each of us had pulled into this very driveway and peeked through the windows, inspired by separate visions of someday, some way, calling this place *home.*

We were driving by on our way to the mine the day we saw the *For Sale* sign on the property. It was the first time either of us mentioned any interest to the other. As if hidden flood gates opened, we schemed and dreamed about the buying the place as we headed toward Harrison Creek. Even though we weren't yet married, we agreed to become partners to see if we could buy the land.

Instead of taking a right at the mine turn-off, we drove past it and on into Central (the nearest phone) so Yukon could call her Dad, who's a Fairbanks Realtor. "We want to buy this place out in Fox," she told him.

"Go dig up some gold to use for a down pay-ment," he replied succinctly. "I'll look into the details of the real estate."

The sluice box was good to us that summer, yielding an agreeable down payment. However the unfinished building would not qualify for any kind of standard loan, so it still took months of negotiating and creative financing to close the deal. Finally, it all came out even. Our mining season ended, and we moved directly into our dream house as newlyweds. Our part-nership had taken on a new dimension.

The deed to our land includes a mineral survey number indicating that this is patented mining ground. Most of the surrounding countryside was mined, first by hand at the turn of the century, then, around 1930, by the big dredges of the Fairbanks Exploration Co. After the heyday of mining passed, the old mining claims were resold as real estate.

A small pup creek called Gold Run divides our property into two sections. All of the ground between the creek and the Steese Highway, including where the house stands, is dredge tailings. We had to bring in top-soil to cover the gravel out front so we could have some semblance of a lawn.

However, while walking our property line we sensed that our land on the other side of Gold Run (almost two acres) had not been mined at all. We made plans to save this dirt for a time we really needed it, maybe even for retirement.

Yukon and I have made a lot of changes to that husk of a house through the years. The interior is still unfinished, or rather it has been refinished several times. Several layers of paint still don't fully hide the messages on recycled signs from political campaigns. A relative once commented that it looked like three different interior designers had been at work here. We like to think of it as user-friendly.

Yukon and I started calling our place "The Biosphere" way before the experiment in Arizona made the idea a laughing matter. We were looking for alternative means of supporting ourselves because every year brought more restrictive mining regulations. We knew of some miners who were successfully growing cranberries in one of their old settling ponds. Could there be other ways to turn these potential liabilities into agricultural assets?

We plotted a course, starting with one word, and the word was *biosphere,* based on the dictionary definition: "the part of the world in which life can exist."

If we were to formulate language suitable for a grant proposal on The Biosphere, it would have read: *To research, review, and apply the steps necessary to extract minerals from a creek bed and convert the resulting tailings to an agriculture status with the ultimate goal of providing a subsistence lifestyle on five acres or less for a family (maximum size to be deter-*

mined by research) in Alaska's Goldstream Valley Basin.

Suppose we could have gotten a grant for this? We never even considered it.

The Biosphere notion was kicked around for a few years until necessity reared its head. We'd been through two very expensive years of legal battles after our little mining operation had been shut down by the government, and we were running out of things to sell. Our limited choices: either mine some of our retirement ground or sell the mining equipment.

Perhaps that precious yellow metal we'd looked for all over the state was right here in our own backyard. If only we had a little operating cash, we could at least run some tests on the ground.

There we were in 1989, just taking stock, when an oil tanker, the *Exxon Valdez,* ran into a rock and made a mess of things in Prince William Sound. The oil company's response to the problem was classical Alaskan Industry: "Throw money at it." Yukon offered our two unemployed nephews a ride down to Valdez, and all three of them joined the oil spill clean-up crews.

Yukon kept sending home those big, money's-no-object checks, and I promptly put them all into a hole in the backyard — we were back in business.

The first test indicated plenty of good gold (*is there such a thing as bad gold?*) but it was buried under fifty feet of overburden. The bottom twenty-five feet of this were wet (meaning below the water table), requiring religious pumping schedules. We built ponds to pump this water into so we could use it for sluicing. A deep hole, nearly one acre in size, left by the dredge as it wallowed in a turn sixty-some years ago, came to fulfill the destiny of any good hole: It was filled in. This new area became the sluicing site, complete with settling ponds to capture the silt and sands. Our one hundred percent total recycle of the water meant we

TRICIA BROWN

Mining the backyard in 1989. Dexter and crew, Bob Jones and Charlie Castro, strike a pose reminiscent of the Gold Rush days.

had zero discharge! One less permit!

The paystreak turned out to be real spotty, then we hit an area entirely void of gold. But on the last day of the season, a three-quarter-ounce nugget caught in the test riffle. Typical mining season — it always gets good at the end.

Aunt Sylvia and Uncle Ed were visiting from Wisconsin that summer. Uncle Ed kept shaking his head, counting the machines and figuring out how much diesel fuel we used every day.

"Why, it's just like farming," he said more than once. "You depend on Mother Nature to provide, and you can never be sure of what she's going to give you."

Until then, I always thought I'd left the farmer in me back on the farm.

The best comment of the summer came from Uncle Gerald, who knew about our trials with the government. When he came out to visit one afternoon, he found me about forty feet in the ground with my back hoe, digging for sixty. As I climbed up to shake his hand, he casually said, "I see you are planting your potatoes a little deeper this year."

"Yeah," I said, taking his cue. "There's this pesky yellow metal in our soil that we have to get out, or else it turns the inside of the potato all yellow like gold. We're just trying to grow bakers."

Mining the first cut was the hinge-pin of our plans for The Biosphere. We needed the settling ponds for basic gardening dirt. The tailings were used to level the sub-soil in preparation for the farming phase. As soon as the gold was removed from a spot, that area could be reconfigured to produce another kind of wealth — the kind you can eat!

Before jet airliners, Alaskans had to grow their own produce, verified by the names of local roads like Farmers Loop, or subdivisions like Garden Island Homes. The Midnight Sun growing season has produced legendary hundred-pound cabbages and enough potatoes to feed the army (literally).

Part of the focus with our Biosphere is to revive and preserve the techniques those old-timers used to adapt their environment to sustain them. Should the next generation have to learn it all the hard way?

For our earliest gardening experiments, I built a false-fronted greenhouse, and we painted it to match the house. The soil came straight out of the settling ponds, so it lacked organic material. Farmers used manure to build up the soil. What we needed were some animals to make us some manure. Rabbits were first, followed over the years by pigs, chickens, more rabbits, goats, turkeys, ducks, a friend's horses for a summer, and rabbits again. It took us a couple of years to get the soil balanced and the greenhouse producing vegetables.

TRICIA BROWN

The Biosphere is home to an extended family of animals, too, including two dogs, a cat, and our housepig, Rosie.

Since we were looking to perpetuate The Biosphere beyond our lifetimes, we invited some relatives to join our endeavor. Three of our older nephews — Rob, Pete, and Paul — answered the call at various times. Only rarely were all three living here, so they took turns staying in our portable bunkhouse unit. Their timing was right-on for the garden plots that required lots of manual labor — picking out rocks, tilling the soil, adding organic garbage and manure, and building raised garden beds.

The garden area has been enlarged to more than a thousand square feet, and another plot approaching that size is growing nearby. The nephews were key to this effort, even hauling in pick-up loads of manure from a local farm. Each of them has gone on to pursue dreams of his own, but every spring, one or another comes nosing around, itching to get a gardening fix.

Even before the boys had moved on, two of their

mothers (my sisters), relocated to participate in our experiment. Vickie came first, bringing along her own one-room log cabin. Sandy moved into and eventually acquired our old mining cook shack building with only three hundred miles on it. Both of them have been a welcome addition, helping with the garden and pitching in with daily chores.

All of our household garbage is still collected in fifty-five-gallon drums averaging about seven drums full per year. We tried composting this in the traditional manner, but our short summers produced an only half-rotted product.

Research revealed a method of trench composting where the raw garbage is deposited right in the ground. The earth piled on top is warmed by the decaying vegetation. This is our preferred method for getting rid of lots of potentially smelly winter garbage build-up. Vegetables can be planted earlier in these warmer soils. Within a year, only beautiful black soil, with maybe a few chicken bones in it, remained in the trench.

The beginnings of fresh, clean food for our table. The raised beds are an absolute necessity in sub-Arctic regions.

TRICIA BROWN

The "pesky yellow stuff" that's in the dirt. I find I have to dig it up to keep it from contaminating the soil for my potatoes.

We learned to add red worms and their castings to the garden every year. Since our harsh winters greatly diminish their population, we move a batch of these earthworms into the furnace room where we feed them garbage all winter.

To ensure proper pollination of our plants, we have recently added honey bees to our menagerie. The first lesson: There is a reason its called bee-keeping, not bee-having. It took two seasons of experience before we managed a small harvest, but there's never been any sweeter honey. Plus, eating raw honey from our bees minimizes the effects of Yukon's spring pollen allergies.

Our best gardening success story has been growing peas. The first year, we had vines and flowers, but not one pea pod. The next year, not one pea made it into the house. There were so few we ate them right in the garden. After ten years of changing varieties and altering soil conditions, recently we achieved a virtual wall of peas more than seven feet tall, greatly exceeding our

TRICIA BROWN

The repair work never ends when you keep a small fleet of classic Chevys. Here, I'm replacing a headlight on the baby blue 1953 model that Yukon drives in the summers. Beyond me is a 1946 in burgundy, and our winter get-around car, a 1951 emerald green Chevy. Two more parts cars are parked out back.

expectations. Now we need to build a sturdier pea fence.

Blue ribbon sweet corn can be grown in the area, but getting a crop to produce edible ears has proven to be our biggest challenge. Any other vegetable that has given us this much problem has long since been dropped from the plan. Next summer will be our seventh try. There's just something about that wonderful taste of fresh sweet corn, calling to mind a boy in a corn field filling grocery bags with gold to give to others. Three dozen ears for a dollar. We'll keep trying.

Upon returning home from the break we took to write this book, we became aware of just how we much appreciate our bio-family. They met us at the airport, and drove us home to a clean, cozy house and well-tended pets. Having family watch the place had given us the peace of mind we needed and eliminated pet-worry syndrome. In the kitchen, the scent of a still-warm pie filled the room with the irresistible aroma of strawberries and home-grown rhubarb. *Thank you, Vickie.*

Yes, they'd even gotten ice cream to go with it. The biggest shock was reaching into the freezer to get the ice cream. Sandy had been through here, too. It takes a person with more strength than I have to clean out somebody else's freezer. Some of that stuff was old enough to carbon date.

Rosie, the mining pig.

As we settled in enjoying hot pie, cold ice cream, and a warm reception, the true meaning of our biosphere was expressed in the well-worn, yet apt phrase: "There's no place like home."

Maybe it is possible to create a biosphere without family, but we don't think so. The one in Arizona is a tourist attraction now. Ours only looks that way. ✿

KEN GRAHAM / KEN GRAHAM AGENCY

Our latest mining endeavor brought us to the Eldorado Gold Mine, where visitors take a train trip through Alaska's mining history, and we share our experiences and expertise in placer mining.

An Unbeatable Pay Streak
By Dexter Clark

There we were, surrounded by ten-year-olds and intimidated beyond imagination. Any prior experience with young children was limited to nieces, nephews and neighbors' kids. Why, we weren't this nervous that time we were surrounded by armed Federal Marshals — but I'll save that story for another book.

"Hey Mister, hey Yukon, is *this* gold?"

Never before had we heard the same question asked so often with such sincerity and eagerness. Is this what parents and teachers go through every day?

I looked down into bright, expectant faces. Little hands held glittering flakes of mica or a yellow, well-oxidized quartz chip. "Sorry, that's not gold," I said. "You've got 'fool's gold.' Keep looking!"

Disappointment crossed their faces for a second, then back to their panning, seeking that magic metal that has been known to drive men mad.

As "real" Alaskan gold miners at the Eldorado Gold Mine, Yukon and I had been asked to meet visitors, talk a little about our experiences, and demonstrate how mining is done today. Then guests would get a chance to pan for gold themselves. These fourth- and fifth-graders were our first visitors at this newly expanded attraction — kind of a dress rehearsal for the three hundred fifty groups we were to welcome during our first season in the visitor industry.

The life of a gold miner has always been shaped

KEN GRAHAM / KEN GRAHAM AGENCY

Yukon circulates around the Eldorado's panning area helping our guests "go for the gold."

and measured by seasons — hard work between break-up and freeze-up, pushing the envelope by building fires in the sluice box to melt the ice — then closing down the camp and looking ahead to the next summer. Should we mine for ourselves or someone else? Would work be available next season?

Together, we had more than thirty years of mining under our belts by the spring of 1994, both as independents and as employees. My prospects for another summer's work at the Fort Knox mine outside Fairbanks were pretty good, but no one was sure just when things would gear up for the construction phase of the new, open pit gold mine.

Just ten miles north of our property, the Fort Knox project was destined to become the largest open-pit gold mine in North America. A good worker could expect the job to last at least ten years, with a handsome retirement package waiting at the bottom of the pit. There was no doubt in our minds that after working with them for three years during the exploration phase, this mine would be a part of our future as well as the future of our small, friendly, community of Fox.

That spring, Yukon and I received a telephone call from Captain Jim Binkley, the patriarch of a Fairbanks family-owned business called Alaska Riverways, Inc. Three generations of Binkleys are engaged in popular riverboat cruises of the Chena and Tanana rivers. He said they were expanding their tour business into gold mining. They wanted a "mining family" who'd be ambassadors for the entire placer gold mining industry in Alaska. He said he'd been asking around town, and our names kept coming up.

We wondered how we would fit in, as actual gold miners, with a project that we assumed was intended to entertain, perhaps even educate, thousands of visitors. Would this be as good an opportunity as mining for the Fort Knox project?

We were impressed by the layout of the operation. A replica of the early Tanana Valley Railroad would bring the guests around to the mine site, and they'd learn about how miners have worked the ground through the last century. We'd show them how it's done today, then they'd get to pan some gold for themselves and keep whatever they found. Our initial assessment — everything was here to make a gold mine. All that they needed was some miners and their equipment. We pledged to give it a try, and with a handshake, we made a three-year commitment.

Yukon and I had our old, reliable Koehring backhoe hauled to the mine to feed the sluice box and do some testing. We set the sluice box as we would have at any other site — except nowhere else had we installed benches for visitors to watch us at work! Our mining experiences were gleaned to develop our presentation. And before there was time for second

The Eldorado has everything for a successful mining operation: pay dirt, a sluice box, moving water, and miners. That's me at the controls of the backhoe, demonstrating how gold mining is done today.

thoughts, that teeming swarm of excited youngsters made us realize we'd made the right decision.

In our first three summers at the Eldorado Gold Mine, we gave more than a thousand presentations to about 150,000 visitors. We also spoke about gold, and how to find it, during classroom visits in Alaska and Hawaii as well as in the Lower 48. Curiosity surely knows no age.

Our visitors asked a few questions so often that we compiled these "fun facts" about the Eldorado:

- *The Eldorado Gold Mine has been in operation on Little Eldorado Creek since the early 1980s.*

- *On an average day, between one and two ounces of gold are panned by each train load of our guests.*

- *On our best day so far, a woman from Iowa found the most gold — $328 worth.*

- *The biggest nugget that a visitor panned from one poke sack had a value of $149.*

- *Gold found here averages eighty-five percent gold and ten percent silver, or approximately 21K.*

- *We have thirty-five combined years of mining experience, spanning five different drainages: Harrison Creek, Maiden Pup, Goldstream, Bonanza Creek, and Gold Run.*

- *The deepest hole we ever worked was fifty-six feet, top to bottom.*

- *In our best "cut," we were getting three ounces per hour of "feeding the box" pay dirt.*

TRICIA BROWN

Gold comes in all sizes, from "fines" to flakes to nuggets. Old-timers say it isn't a nugget unless it plinks in the pan.

- *Biggest nugget we ever found: two and one-half ounces, in the test riffle at the Eldorado.*

- *We are open when the water thaws until freeze-up — mid-May to mid-September.*

- *Of ninety-two acres in the entire operation, most is second-growth aspen and birch.*

- *It takes almost forty full-time employees to keep things running.*

- *The logs in the cook shack and panning area are Tanana Valley white spruce. Nearly three thousand linear feet of whole logs were used in the buildings.*

- *More than 2,500 spruce ties are used on the rail bed.*

- *The mile-long track is recycled Alaska Railroad rail steel from the 1920s.*

- *Our small locomotive is a replica of an 1899 Porter 0-4-0; also the original engine of the Tanana Valley Railroad that came out here to the Goldstream Valley until the late 1920s.*

- *Most of the power comes from a 90-horsepower, 6-cylinder, Duetz diesel concealed in the wood car; hydraulics transfer the power to its wheels.*

- *The three hundred-foot-long permafrost tunnel was excavated down through permafrost (permanently frozen soil) during construction. The walls of rein-forced concrete and steel give an example of the strata in this area, where gold is found, and how it was deposited there.*

- *The "Cookie Jar" in Fairbanks makes us almost a quarter-million cookies per season.*

We've enjoyed our summers at the Eldorado so much, it looks like we're in for the long haul. And as seasonal workers, knowing where we'll be mining each year is a bonus in itself!

Like I told Captain Jim one day, "This is the best pay streak we've ever worked." ✿

TRICIA BROWN

Placer gold is distinctive in color and brightness. Interior Alaska miners, assayers, and jewelers often can examine a nugget and name the creek or area from which it was mined.

GOLD!
Where to Find It, How to Pan It
By Dexter Clark

Where is the best place to look for gold?

The first answer is always, "Gold is where you find it, and seldom where you look." We look for many signs. The first clue is evidence of old diggings. We have yet to find any gold where there were no signs of previous mining activity. The old-timers usually had taken out what we call the "gut" of the pay streak. Depending on where the river or creek (water) was running when the most gold was eroding out of the mountain, the pay streak meanders like a creek itself.

To either side of the "gut" is the rim pay, the term used to describe the gold old-timers left at either edge of the pay streak. There's no profit in this gold at $16 or even $32 per ounce, yet many a modern-day placer miner makes his livelihood working these leavings.

The next clue is to look for any natural interference with the flow of the stream, such as a bend in the river or a hard rocky point jutting into the stream. Anything that would cause the water to slow down, and let go of its load of gravel and gold, is worth checking.

The next step is to dig a deep hole, as close to bedrock as possible. Check the surface gravel and each subsequent layer (about a foot apart) for gold using the techniques in the "how to pan" section that follows.

How did the gold get into the creeks and streams in the first place?

This answer requires a little amateur geology

lesson. Picture a volcano that never made it to the surface of the earth. This hot molten rock and mineral mix (magma) is trapped in what is called a magma chamber. When the natural forces that formed the magma chamber begin to subside, and the molten rocks and minerals begin to cool, the rocks start to solidify. A green stone called olivine is the first to gel. Since a solid is more dense than a liquid, it settles to the bottom.

Five other major rock types cool and precipitate out. The last rock to cool is the pretty white quartz. While this process is under way, the minerals are still in a near gaseous state and being lighter, have risen to the very top of the chamber. Our geology teacher called these "the good juices." Gold, silver, platinum, copper, lead, zinc, and other metallic minerals can be found here.

Before everything cools completely, some external natural force may exert another form of pressure on the magma chamber, an earthquake for example. The result is the pushing and squeezing of the semi-liquid quartz and good juices out into the cracks and weak places in the earth's crust. As the gold and silver invades the country rock, it begins to cool and solidify, forming the little mineralized veins of gold-bearing quartz ore sought by the hard rock miner.

It takes thousands of years for the gold that was formed up in the mountains to be eroded away by the forces of nature, then washed down into the stream bed along with the rocks, sand and gravel. Since gold is more than nineteen times heavier than water, the majority of the placer gold we seek is found toward the bottom of this gravel. Under the gravel is the bedrock, so-called because it is not moving downstream along with the gravel. The gold will work its way into the bedrock as far down as there are cracks to hide in.

We find the most gold in the last two feet of gravel and the first two feet of the bedrock.

Why doesn't placer gold all look the same?

The size of the flakes and nuggets of gold varies from one creek to another. The nature and the age of the original deposit, the method and time of erosion, and many other factors affect the gold's condition.

Different creeks, or drainages, as we call them, will have different qualities and quantities of gold. We have worked areas where the gold dust and flakes averaged seventy to seventy-five percent gold and fifteen to twenty percent silver. Most of the gold nugget jewelry sold in the Eldorado gift shop averages between eight-five to ninety-five percent gold.

To convert to karat value (diamonds are weighed in carats), we know that 24K is pure gold or a fineness of 99.9 percent gold. This is what the assayer means when he says "three nines fine." So 12K gold is fifty percent gold. Since pure gold is relatively soft and malleable, many other metals are used to alloy the gold to give it strength and to keep the gold from wearing away quickly. With white gold, nickel is the main alloy.

An assayer with a practiced eye can tell which area or drainage gold came from just by looking at it. The nuggets will have different physical characteristics such as color and shape. The color is an indicator of the purity so a high silver content will lighten the gold's color considerably. The shape reveals a lot about the geology of the formation of the gold. The flatter gold is usually older and has traveled farther.

Which is heavier, a pound of butter or a pound of gold?

Within the English units of measurement there are three different systems of weights (avoirdupois, troy, and apothecaries'), of which the most widely used is the avoirdupois. The troy system (named for Troyes, France, where it is said to have originated) is used only for precious metals. Apothecaries' weights are based on

Yukon and her gold made the feature pages of her hometown newspaper recently when she visited Kankakee, Illinois.

troy weights; in addition to the pound, ounce, and grain — which are equal to the troy units of the same name. Other units are the dram and the scruple.

A pound of butter is weighed in avoirdupois weight in which:

1 pound = 16 ounces
1 ounce = 28 grams
1 grain = .0648 gram
1 pound = 16 ounces = 7,000 grains = 454 grams

Gold is weighed in troy weight in which:

1 pound = 12 ounces
1 ounce = 480 grains
1 grain = .0648 gram
1 pound = 12 ounces = 5760 grains = 373 grams

The pound of butter is 81 grams, or 2,240 grains, or 2.9 ounces (of butter) heavier. ✿

How to Pan for Gold

While panning tools and techniques may vary from "speed" panning at a cut, to careful sorting of screened concentrates, the basic process is the same any where in the world.

When you're learning to pan, it's best to practice with concentrates — that way you're guaranteed that there will be gold in the pan. Almost any gift shop in Alaska offers some sort of "panning kit," or if you're really lucky, you may be able to find a local miner willing to sell you some of his concentrates.

If you don't have a creek running through your backyard, the hardest part about panning might be finding a suitable washtub or receptacle for the tailings (concentrates after the gold is removed). It's a good idea to recover the tailings and check for overlooked gold the first couple times you try panning.

Next you need a gold pan, or mineral bowl as they are technically called. Failing all else, a pie dish can be used. Your tub needs to be bigger around than your gold pan. A conventional washtub works best, but you could use a baby bathtub, dishpan, bread bowl, child's wading pool, etc. Since the sands and gravel will clog the drain, the kitchen sink is not a good choice unless you line the sink with a strong garbage bag.

Here's a step-by-step look at panning procedure:

1. Set up a staging area. Outside is best if the weather is nice. Remember you will be working with water. Scrape together the following items:
   * A bag of store-bought concentrates or other potentially gold-laden material
   * Gold pan, mineral bowl, or pie dish
   * Washtub or other suitable container
   * Enough water to half-fill the tub

Step 1. Pour paydirt into pan.   *Step 2. Fill with water, tilt pan, start to wash away top layer.*

* Container for your gold (an old film canister works well)
* Useful optional equipment: tweezers or knife

2. Depending on the depth of your tub, fill it half or three-quarters full of water. It is hard to pan in less than four inches of water.

3. Start with about one cupful of dirt if you are using concentrates. Fill your pan no more than half full if using river gravel.

4. With the dirt in the pan, and looking down into a tub of water, keep the pan level, submerge it, and fill it with water. Bring it up out of the water, and shake and rotate the pan in a circular motion until all of the dirt is completely wet and very soupy.

5. While stirring the soup, break up any clumps of dirt or clay with your fingers. Remove the very largest stones, inspecting them to make sure they are clean, and set them aside or discard them.

6. Get the dirt really soupy again, and start tipping the pan while making the soup. Don't allow any of the stone soup to work over the edge. The idea is to center the soupy dirt over the deepest part of the pan. The angle of the pan is such that most of the water runs out.

7. Holding the pan at that same angle, dip it straight into the water, allowing a little wave of water to come into the pan, then quickly raise it so the same

Step 3. Remove larger stones.   ***Step 4. Go back to the "beach" and tip the pan at this angle.***

wave washes back out, taking with it some of the lighter surface sands and gravel that contains no gold. If you start with two tablespoons of concentrates, the wave effect is more obvious with less material in the pan.

8. After washing away a little of the top layer, allow the material to settle in as single a layer as possible (another good reason to start with less than a full pan of dirt). Look for larger stones to pick out, as you get farther along in your panning, the big rocks keep getting smaller. Some of these rocks have the typical white quartz in them. The shiny, sparkly, flat-sided stones are mostly mica-schist.

9. Next take up some water and make it soupy again. The gold that may have moved up by the wave action will go back to the bottom of the pan.

10. Re-center the soup over the deepest part of the pan, allowing the water to run out slowly. Then go back to the beach — dip, dip, dip. Each little dip brings in a wave of water that, like at the beach, picks up a few of the lighter sands and gravel, and carries them back into the tub with each wave.

Repeat steps 8, 9, and 10. Each time there should be less material in the pan. Work the pile smaller and smaller until there's a tablespoon or two of dirt left.

11. Puddle this dirt over the deepest part of the pan and carefully pour out any remaining water. Now

 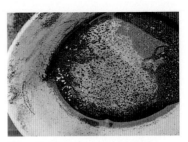

Step 5. Swirl the pan to separate the lighter material.   ***Step 6. Pick out your gold.***

the tricky part: Without disturbing your pile, tilt your pan to let in about a half cup of water on the opposite side from the dirt.

12. Holding the pan level, slowly swirl the small amount of water by tipping the pan, as if there were a marble or small steel ball in there and you're trying to roll it around the base of the pan. Think of the water as a marble, just roll it around the bottom. Each time the water passes over the pile, a little of the surface layer should be washed across the bottom of the pan and allowed to settle on the opposite side. Then initiate another swirl of water to gently wash away another layer. Repeat.

By this time, even a few crude swirls should reveal any gold that is in the pan. If you started with a small amount of dirt and there's no gold in it, don't get discouraged. Try a little more dirt, saving the tailings to check for gold once you get the knack.

13. After you've washed the dirt off your gold, it is easy to pick up with tweezers. If no tweezers are handy, a dry finger will pick up damp gold unless the gold is actually in some water. Try it, it works. Then a little tap of your finger, and the gold pops off into a film canister or other container you've chosen.

And finally, give yourself a pat on the back with our congratulations! You're a gold miner! ✿

A ROCKY AND GOLDEN GLOSSARY

Alloy Mixing of gold with one or more metals (i.e. silver, zinc, nickel, copper, etc.) to produce varying characteristics and color. Because pure gold is soft, it is alloyed to make it more durable.

Assay A test to determine the amount of gold in an alloy.

Cat Slang for heavy equipment manufactured by Caterpillar, Inc., and a generic term for any bulldozer, regardless of manufacturer or color. Also called *crawler* in miner's slang, i.e.: "Why are Terex crawlers painted green? So they can hide in the woods when a real bulldozer (a bright yellow Caterpillar) comes along!"

Claim A tract of land staked out for the purpose of removing a valuable mineral from it. A gold mining claim is generally twenty acres.

Crawler See **Cat**.

Cut The area from which the miner removes gold. Also called "the pit."

Deposit A natural accumulation, such as a deposit of gold in a stream bed.

Dirt Gravel, rocks, sand, silt, clays, and earth of any kind that is being mined, especially pay dirt that is dumped in the sluice. See **Sluice**.

Dozer Short form of bulldozer.

Dump bed The top end of the sluice box where the pay dirt is dumped to begin the washing process.

Fool's gold Common name for iron pyrite. Unlike gold,

which is malleable, iron pyrite is very brittle.

Gold *Au* Atomic number 79; atomic weight 196.967. A soft, yellow metallic element that is malleable and resistent to corrosion.

Gold-filled The covering of base metal objects with a layer of gold.

Gold Fever A non-medical term used to describe the mental and physical effects of the craving for gold.

Gold Rush A large-scale influx of gold prospectors to an area where gold has recently been found. The first result is a dramatic increase in population. Some of the more famous of the gold rushes were in 1849 at Sutter's Mill, California; in 1952 at New South Wales and Victoria, Australia; in the 1880s in Rhodesia; in 1886 at Forty-mile Creek, Yukon Territory, Canada; in 1886 at Johannesburg, South Africa; in 1886 at Kimberly, West Australia; and from 1897 through 1898 in the great Klondike River Valley, Yukon Territory, Canada.

Grizzly A component of the sluice used to keep the larger rocks from entering the dump bed area of the sluice. A simple grizzly can be made from parallel steel bars, five to eight inches apart, place at right angles to the dump bed.

Karat A measure of the amount of gold in an alloy. One karat is equal to 1/24th part of pure gold. 24K is 100 percent pure gold.

Lode Gold-bearing masses of rock that are still in place, even though they may be weathered.

Lower 48 Alaskan slang for the continental U.S.

Outside Alaskan slang for anyplace that's not Alaska.

Overburden Topsoil and gravel deposited on top of a paystreak. Doesn't hold enough gold to mine at profit.

Pay dirt Soil, gravel, or ore that yields a profit to a miner.

Paystreak Area of a creek bottom that contains enough gold to be mined at a profit. In placer mining, the equivalent of the vein sought by the hard rock miner. The paystreak may meander like an unseen creek, be concentrated in a glory hole, or end abruptly.

Pit Where the mining is taking place; same meaning as "the cut" to a miner.

Placer gold Gold deposits that were left in the creek bed along with gravel and sand during the erosion of solid rocks from a gold vein. Also called "free gold."
  gold dust The smallest size of recoverable placer gold; varies in size from flour to sugar granules.
  gold flakes Placer gold pieces, larger than dust, that have been beaten flat during the erosion process.
  gold nuggets The larger pieces of placer gold. The old timers used to say, "If it plinks in the pan, it's a nugget." The largest gold nugget ever found was the Holterman Nugget. Weighing nearly six hundred pounds, it was found in Australia in 1857.

Prospect Used as a noun, it is a place showing signs of containing a mineral deposit, the mineral yield of a tested sample of ore or gravel, or a likely candidate. As a verb, it means to look for gold or other minerals.

Riffles Component of the sluice that traps the gold. The most common riffles are made of angle iron.

Settling pond Containment area for muddy water allowing the dirt to settle out before the water is returned to the stream.

Slick plate The area between the dump bed and the main sluice where the gold starts to go to the bottom of the slurry, preparing it for the riffles.

Slurry Mixture of water with gravel, silt, sand, and clay.

Sluice or sluice box The devise used by gold miners to concentrate the pay dirt. A typical sluice box is two to three feet wide and thirty to fifty feet long with sides measuring one or two feet high. The components of a sluice, starting at the top, include: The grizzly or other screening device to keep out large rocks, the dump bed, the slick plate, and the box itself. Along the floor of the box are the riffles. Beneath the riffles are the mats, usually made from artificial turf used in sports stadiums.

Solid gold Refers to gold that is 24K and contains no other metals. Also referred to as "three nines fine" meaning 99.9 percent gold.

Sourdough Slang for long-time resident, and especially an old-time prospector in Alaska or northwest Canada.

Troy ounce Common unit for measuring precious metals. One troy ounce is ten percent heavier than the more common avoirdupois ounce. ✿